She Sheds Style

MAKE YOUR SPACE YOUR OWN

ERIKA KOTITE

COOL
SPRINGS
PRESS

Inspiring | Educating | Creating | Entertaining

Brimming with creative inspiration, how-to projects, and useful information to enrich your everyday life, Quarto Knows is a favorite destination for those pursuing their interests and passions. Visit our site and dig deeper with our books into your area of interest: Quarto Creates, Quarto Cooks, Quarto Homes, Quarto Lives, Quarto Drives, Quarto Explores, Quarto Gifts, or Quarto Kids.

First published in 2018 by Cool Springs Press, an imprint of The Quarto Group,
401 Second Avenue North, Suite 310, Minneapolis, MN 55401 USA.
T (612) 344-8100 F (612) 344-8692 www.QuartoKnows.com

Cool Springs Press titles are also available at discount for retail, wholesale, promotional, and bulk purchase. For details, contact the Special Sales Manager by email at specialsales@quarto.com or by mail at The Quarto Group, Attn: Special Sales Manager, 401 Second Avenue North, Suite 310, Minneapolis, MN 55401 USA.

10 9 8 7 6 5 4 3 2

ISBN: 978-0-7603-6099-6

Library of Congress Cataloging-in-Publication Data

Names: Kotite, Erika, 1962- author.
Title: She sheds style : make your space your own / Erika Kotite.
Description: Minneapolis, MN, USA : Cool Springs Press,
an imprint of The Quarto Group, 2018. | Includes bibliographical references and index.
Identifiers: LCCN 2018008213 | ISBN 9780760360996 (plc)
Subjects: LCSH: Sheds--Design and construction--Amateurs' manuals. |
Interior decoration--United States. | Women--Homes and haunts--United States.
Classification: LCC NA8301 .K68 2018 | DDC 747/.88922--dc23
LC record available at https://lccn.loc.gov/2018008213

Acquiring Editor: Thom O'Hearn
Project Manager: Alyssa Bluhm
Art Director and Cover Design: Cindy Samargia Laun
Page Design: Shubhani Sarker and Diana Boger
Layout: Diana Boger

Printed in China

MIX
Paper from
responsible sources
FSC® C016973

Contents

Introduction

A Style of Our Own

IN SHE SHEDS: *A Room of Your Own,* the owners of these wonderful little structures each came forth with personal details about how they built and used their she sheds. Launching from this intimate introduction into the wonderful world of artfully built private spaces comes a new phase: giving your she shed its own distinctive style.

Can a she shed truly have style? Of course it can! Style simply means a particular look based on cohesive design principles—or even not so cohesive. In fact, as more and more she sheds spring to life and are shared via social media, they are beginning to drive a nascent style of their own. Style applies both to the exterior and its architectural elements and to interior considerations. Often the two dance together, celebrating the intrinsic utilitarian nature of a shed while acknowledging its pretty new clothing. The she shed revels in its emerging status as the best private getaway of our age.

In fact, sheds are a lot of fun to decorate for many reasons. They are small, so the risk of trying something new is lower. They thrive with castoff pieces and thrifty flea market finds. They're the place we finally can indulge in that periwinkle door we've always wanted. They can hold our stuff yet still be beautiful to behold.

Sheds enjoy a rare iconic status close to that of an actual house. We see them and instantly know what they are and what they're used for. Yes, they have the humble reputation of serving as a catchall—an extra garage, if you will. That humble and utilitarian aspect remains a strong thread in the design tapestry and shouldn't be left out. Shelving, alcoves, lofts, and built-ins are standard fare on the inside, while sturdy foundations, walls, and roofs keep the shed protected throughout the seasons.

In this book we'll discuss a variety of styles, but whatever style you choose, I encourage you to make it your own. Take your time to build a style that speaks to who you are. Build and decorate a she shed that satisfies some inner yearning you've had for a long, long time. This is your chance to really think about the colors and elements you like to surround yourself with. Leather camp chair or slipcovered easy chair, exotic Oriental rug or cheerful rag rug made with your favorite old pajamas: the choices are all yours. Play around with the unfamiliar, but don't ever feel bad about choosing the familiar. This book is all about "no rules."

What You'll Find

Get ready to roll up your sleeves, because this book offers dozens of projects from start to finish, starting in Chapter 2, along with helpful tips and alternatives. Women are creating such amazing and ingenious components to make their she sheds unique; some of these might be perfect for yours too. With these projects, you can try to copy them exactly, borrow a couple of steps and drop everything else, change materials or colors, or simply use them as inspiration—it's all according to your needs. You will end up understanding how to bring a shed from plain to just plain dazzling, using color, architectural elements, clever landscaping, and brilliant interior design. Just as important, you'll learn a little bit more about who you are in the process. You have some fun times ahead!

1 | *She Sheds: The Elements of Style*

For most of your life, the backyard shed was a barely noticed, plain little structure that housed Dad's yard tools and maybe the family's plastic kiddie pool. It was ugly, boring, and ignored. Who would have ever predicted that this ordinary little utility shed of childhood would become a celebrated woman's place of beauty and repose?

It's incredible to see how in just a few years, sheds have earned a lofty status, offering potential for an enhanced property, extra room for living and working, and an attractive element that adds to rather than detracts from the backyard landscape.

Now is the time of the she shed. Women have discovered a convenient and practical solution to their problem: how to procure their own space conveniently and affordably. Sheds are truly the new frontier for discovering creative potential and recapturing sanity in a busy life. Turning a no-frills structure made for

Modern, cheerful, and artsy, Kirsty Patrick's shed is a perfect marriage of form and function. A busy entrepreneur with a growing artisanal light fixture business, Kirsty made budget choices—an old door made over into a table and chipboard wall paneling—that nevertheless convey an ultra-chic aesthetic.

inanimate objects into a living space encompasses a journey of innovation and vision.

A shed becomes a she shed when it is created, used, and loved by a woman. It can be an old shed given a new life, or a brand-new studio designed by one of the many specialty shed companies, arriving preassembled in the backyard. A woman can build it herself or she may have lots of help. The important point comes with the addition of personal style. Your she shed style will emerge as you consider how you'll be using your shed and the important things you want to surround yourself with. This chapter explores the wonderful ways women are using and styling their she sheds.

Functional and Fabulous

The raison d'être of a she shed is as unique as the woman who owns it. Nevertheless, sheds lend themselves to several specific work and leisure pursuits. Enchanted by the beautiful spaces found online, we each say to ourselves, "I've got to have one of these," without really thinking through what we'd use it for. However, you should get serious with yourself and truthfully answer the following question: "Will I really use a she shed?"

The she shed is a commitment, not only in the time and resources spent building it but also in its continuous use and upkeep. Structures will languish quickly if they don't have regular human habitation; no one is around to see the problems and take care of them. If you have a special place in your home already or few distractions to pull you outdoors, then think long and hard about your decision. Keep in mind, however, that there are other ways to use a she shed even if the house is your domain. Would you like to enhance your backyard so that it is a more welcoming hangout for you and your friends? A she shed will contribute to a new backyard design, but it still should be used and well tended.

What follows are the most common ways she sheds are used and enjoyed, but there are many others; a shed makes a great yoga or meditation room, a pottery-making studio, or even a sound studio for musicians.

Artistry

The artist's atelier has a reserved space in the collective imagination. There are good reasons why artists need their space—creating art is messy, demanding, and often a solitary pursuit. Whether you paint on canvas or do mixed media, a separate studio is valuable because it gives you room and a quiet space to work. Another huge benefit is the ability to leave your work and supplies out instead of cleaning up at the end of each day.

Artistry need not be confined to "fine art." It may take the form of other creative pursuits, such as sewing, quilt-

She sheds are like sirens, drawing us in and allowing us to mentally move in without a second thought. If you are one of the serious ones, then you'll need a plan, starting with what you intend to use it for.

ing, jewelry making, or ceramics. These all require a certain amount of space to work, organize, and store supplies—and, of course, to display the finished work.

A shed tends to work well for artwork. It can be adapted to offer plentiful natural light, if needed. Its practical and durable surfaces are meant to get dirty and clean up easily. (Chalk that one up to potting shed ancestry.) And, finally, a shed's simplicity is harmonious with the relatively stimulating activity of making art.

(Left) The primary activity in this shed is artist Rachel Roe painting on canvas. Much of the main area is taken up with easels, supplies, and a worksurface; a small loft above provides a resting place. The shed is located in Missouri, where it gets cold in the winter. Rachel and her husband chose to drywall and insulate it so she could use it year-round.

A queen bed fits snugly into Vicki Sakioka's she shed. It affords a handy guest room for friends and the occasional exchange student. Vicki's gentle feminine styling is a dramatic transformation for this large old shed, intended originally for storing automotive parts.

Extra Room

Cozy shed-style rooms are the latest movement in the country's most popular online short-term lodging companies. Considering your backyard as a place to create extra revenue is a significant endeavor. Many people have successfully converted old sheds or built new ones as adjunct lodging with great success, but there are many zoning rules and restrictions to follow.

The she shed is by definition a personal space, so the ins and outs of commercial lodging will not be covered here. Instead, let's discuss the function of a she shed as a de facto guest house for those times when you are short on rooms for overnight (non-paying) guests. (Of course, the shed can also double as a built-in nap room for yourself!)

The restful she shed has a daybed or a comfortable sofa as its dominant feature. You may consider laying plumbing for a bathroom, and sheds are usually wired for light and power. If a bathroom isn't possible, then the shed should be positioned close enough to the main house to make using the bathroom convenient. Think about cabinets to store bedding and a small closet area for guests' clothing.

Make it comfortable for others, and make it wonderful for yourself.

Gardening

The humble potting shed, ubiquitous within the allotments of the United Kingdom and in the rambling yards of the East, South, and Midwest, is no doubt the grandmother of she sheds. The potting shed often had a modicum of charm even in the midst of dirt and plant cuttings. Most are spacious enough to house a potting bench and a place to sit down. Potted seedlings and houseplants needing a bit of nursing add their own style to the place.

Chicken coops were not designed for humans, and yet they too helped identify the she shed style. Caring for chickens often has been the woman's responsibility in a farm family. She strives to make the structure a cheery place, painting it barn red, perhaps, or making a pretty sign. The interplay of form and function in the outbuildings used by women has a long history.

Light, bright, and airy, Carla Fisher's potting shed also exhibits the design principles of a greenhouse, with its polycarbonate roof and bank of windows. Ample workspace runs along three of the four walls, and Carla installed a long metal curtain rod to hold hanging plants.

Anita Rackerby's old-time chicken coop is just about as cute as a she shed; a pathway leads from it to Anita's grander shed. Chicken coops have a strong historic tie with she sheds, because they were mainly the farm wife's domain.

A busy interior designer, Alexis King wanted to work from home but still have a separate room where the dedicated space allowed her creativity to run freely. She can also see clients here and maintain a professional atmosphere.

Home Office

For a woman running a business or telecommuting, the shed provides many of the advantages a separate office does, with some additional benefits. In a shed, the office is close to home without being as prone to distractions or interruption. It is an affordable alternative to leasing a space (although you will need to get it wired up for electricity and Wi-Fi, as well as installing heating and air-conditioning). It is private and quiet, and it lets you keep an eye on your house, even while you're at the office.

Using the shed as an office space will require careful planning. Ideally, the workspace—consisting of a worktop, file drawers, shelves, and cabinets—will be versatile enough to serve double duty as a creative area on weekends.

Being inside the shed for a full workday calls for optimum comfort, which includes investing in an ergonomic chair, perhaps a stand-up desk platform, plenty of natural light and/or task and overhead lighting, and well-placed wall sockets for a computer, printer, and other appliances, such as a coffee maker or electric tea kettle.

Social Space

Yes, it's personal and private, but the well-appointed she shed is going to attract attention—and visitors. People fall in love with these backyard structures and want to be around them. This is a good thing and doesn't mean you've lost your privacy. The shed acts more as a backdrop than a party house; it's very useful as a makeshift bar, and the area surrounding it makes for an attractive, defined gathering spot.

Another way to go is to embrace your shed as a friend magnet and a wonderful, small private club. Opening your doors to happy hour with friends, or tea parties with the grandchildren, will get an enthusiastic response. A she shed as entertaining space, then, will be light, bright, and spacious. It should offer a welcoming transition between indoors and outdoors, such as a deck and double doors that open wide. Plan for storage cabinets and (if possible) a food prep area. This kind of social shed should be somewhat close to the house for conveniently transporting dishware and food.

The social shed easily turns back into a private space once the party's over. Just know that it will be more difficult to recapture that "it's all mine" feeling when you let others into the she shed. Sharing the joy of the shed versus keeping it sacred at all times? Listen to your heart.

Writing

Whether you are a professional writer or someone who enjoys journaling in the late afternoon, the act of writing calls for intense concentration. Minutes will swirl past as you craft and rework your paragraphs, until the rude thud of a door flung open signals your quiet time is over. Writing in a shed provides hours of alone time, not to mention pretty views of the yard to inspire and refresh the mind.

The shed is completely detached from the house; not only does that discourage needless interruptions from children and other family members, but it also keeps you away

With just 36 square feet to work with, I had to find a chair that was small enough yet comfortable enough for all the reading I plan to do. This ladies' balloon chair, a piece I've had for years, was a good fit, and I added a small footstool for comfort.

When your she shed is all windows, doors, and drop-down bars, then you know where the party gets started. Amy Smith built her shed from scratch and by herself. She loves opening it up to friends and family for impromptu gatherings; there are plenty of places to sit and socialize both inside and outside.

from impulsive chore-hopping. Your time will be managed more wisely if you have the physical detachment that a writing shed provides.

A desk or table is typically used for writing, although some writers have their own unique places and ways to practice their craft. That might be prone on the floor, stom-ach down, or it could be feet up on a favorite sofa, laptop on lap. As a writer, you'll want to think about your favorite working position and make that a priority when designing the shed. Perhaps a comfortable area rug is more important than a desk.

You Are the Designer

Women are geniuses for identifying sheds as the new life-style frontier. No other building marries scale, convenience, usefulness, affordability, and charm in quite the same way as this humble little outbuilding. That's why building a style genre around the livability of a shed is so exciting.

Being the designer of your she shed should feel thrilling and liberating—there should be no fear whatsoever. So, the moment things start feeling too formal or restrictive, sit down on the nearest comfortable chair and say to yourself, "It is only a shed, but it is *my* shed." Take a deep breath and peruse your favorite Instagram or Pinterest she shed feeds to get the joy back.

If you strive to keep fun and personal satisfaction at the forefront of everything you do, then your shed's style will fall into place. Use the advice and design categories in the chapters ahead for navigation only; they are tools, not rules. Keeping your "buckets" organized is just a way to make the styling job less overwhelming.

Every Inch Counts

Scale is a vital topic that will be covered substantially from an architectural standpoint in Chapter 2. But it's going to be so important in the design and decorating of your shed.

The dimensions of a shed are pretty close to the size of a single room in a house, and yet that room needs to feel like a complete home. It needs to satisfy all the necessities of a human being who is living in that place and under-taking some specific activities. If you are familiar with the principles of tiny house living, you'll see the similarities. Tiny home design has become very sophisticated, using space-saving techniques inspired by recreational vehicles and ship galleys.

Sheds have lower ceilings and smaller footprints, so the lamp that looks fabulous near an oversized sectional is going to overtake a small shed. On the other hand, sometimes a single large "statement" piece is a much better design decision than lots of little ones. Keep scale in mind and measure carefully when building or furnishing, but let your creative intuition speak to you as well.

Design for Comfort

Comfort is strongly connected to scale and space planning, because your shed needs to allow for ease of movement. Depending on the size of a she shed, there will either be plenty of space for all the furnishings, or you might have trouble getting it all positioned without tripping over table legs.

The writer's she shed is often both private and light-filled. In this French-inspired shed, an old-fashioned desk, painted pink, offers enough space for a laptop or journal and looks out over the best views from the shed.

This old potting shed was already on the property when Liz Ridgway and her husband moved in. It's perfectly sound and sturdy but retains its rustic, no-nonsense exterior. Inside, the shed is comfortable and cheerful, outfitted with a workbench, small table, and many gardening, textile, and design books.

For the generous-sized shed, it's still a good idea to do some careful space planning. A larger shed allows you to build in a comfortable sitting/lounging area that will be well situated for light and view. Face the daybed or loveseat toward a French door or opposite a wall with a large window. Most sheds aren't big enough to have a central area for grouping furniture, so it is very important to use wall space wisely. Keep one wall windowless to use for taller furniture, or design windows higher up near the roof.

Refined or Rough around the Edges?

Choosing the kind of shed you'll build can go in two directions: refined or rough. A refined shed is one that mimics a home build in the sense that it is completely finished and trimmed out with standard materials. This shed is completely sealed and has insulation and drywall, baseboards and other finish trim, electrical hardwiring, contractor-grade doors and windows, rain gutters, and vents. New sheds, made from a kit or using all new materials and contractor-level building techniques, are refined sheds. They will be more expensive, but they will exude a very sophisticated sense of permanence. They will also be very comfortable year-round.

The sheds I call "rough around the edges" are most often built by hand and from scratch, often using a lot of mismatched salvaged materials. A lot of love and care are put into the construction, and of course proper measures are taken to ensure a sturdy structure—solid foundation, good building techniques using the right load-bearing lumber, and secure doors and windows. But the walls are not drywalled, and a few things may not be perfectly sealed or level. Rough sheds have the charm of being handcrafted, with the unique feel of outbuildings from long ago.

These are two completely different looks that come with their own pros and cons. Sometimes the decision is made for you by building code laws or the type of weather in your area. Still, you can design with the refined or rough sensibility in mind, using that vision to inform your decisions.

Adding Style to a Kit Shed

Kit shed manufacturers have come a long way in the last few years. Recognizing that many of their customers were buying sheds for small backyard getaways, some companies have started to market their larger and fancier sheds as she sheds. While this is good news, keep in mind that a kit shed only goes so far in its aesthetic and quality level. The sheds are fabricated for a mass market as well as for affordability and efficient transport—they often lack the more substantial details you have in mind.

A kit shed is a great way to get the basic size and shape shed that you want. It's up to you to furnish the stylish add-ons and details. On the next page are some key ways to do this.

This kit shed (inset) was designed for tool storage and didn't include any side windows. Two high-end windows, along with a creative paint scheme and a couple of entry steps, gave the finished version a lot of curb appeal.

Rachel and Ryan Roe added this handy overhang to the side of her storage-turned-she-shed. With its generous metal roof and gravel patio area, the place becomes a welcoming area for relaxing alone or with friends.

- **Change out the windows.** The number one improvement for maximum impact is upgrading and/ or adding windows to a kit shed. Gather your windows and then modify the framework to fit them in. On the inside, building windowsills will add interest to plain walls.
- **Invest in a great door.** If your kit door needs improvement, consider adding small window panels. Make sure the door can allow the necessary framing and support for windows. Otherwise, swap out the kit doors for French doors or a track door.
- **Anchor the shed.** The trouble with plain boxy sheds is that they seem awkward and detached from the rest of the landscape. There are lots of ways to make a shed harmonious with its surroundings. First, choose the site carefully so that the shed connects to a landscape element—perhaps on a slight rise, at the end of a natural pathway, or nestled in a copse of trees. Connect the shed visually to its site using architectural additions, such as a pergola or finished porch. Always make an extra effort to create an attractive front

The Roes' shed was built using purchased plans that called for a rather flat facade. Rachel and Ryan built a handsome awning made with wood and a metal roof that matches the shed roof. The awning, along with a side overhang, completely transformed the original design.

Even the narrow transom window in Debbie Lisee's she shed has great detail—divided lites, with generous sills and trim. The attention given to even humble architectural elements does not go unnoticed.

There are many amazing vinyl and laminate flooring products on the market to choose from. You'll find they work very well in the shed, as they are both pretty and durable. Look for interesting wide-plank profiles that have a nice distressed finish, like this easy and inexpensive laminate floor.

entrance. Bank the shed with plenty of flowerbeds, raised planter boxes, and interesting sculpture.

- **Upgrade the trim.** Customize your trim to a wider or narrower width around windows, corners, and doors. For a unique rustic look, use a better-quality wood and stain it to complement the siding color.

- **Add exciting siding.** Kit shed siding usually consists of thin pre-painted panels that can appear more like vinyl than wood. Substantial trim profiles will improve the look of this siding, as will a couple coats of your own paint. Another great look is shingle siding; it works for many architectural styles, from modern to rustic. You can also invest in clapboard or board and batten siding for a complete makeover.

- **Install a custom floor.** Most kits do not come with flooring material; they'll only provide a frame for it. The simplest of floors would be ¾" or ⅝" plywood that you can paint decoratively. A plain kit shed gets a terrific boost from a stylish floor, whether it's laminate that looks like wood, vinyl plank flooring, or real wood planks.

- **Add dimension to the face.** Sheds look best with an extended overhang, when the roofing extends past the wall by at least 6" (it's also better rain protection). If your kit shed doesn't have an overhang, then consider building a nice wood or metal awning above the door, as a kind of "eyebrow" for the face.

- **Install built-in shelving.** Freestanding furniture is fun because it's eclectic and you can move it around. For the plain Jane shed, however, adding built-ins will really make a big difference. Why? The shelves turn bare walls into design elements. If you paint them the same color as the walls, you achieve a cohesive and nuanced backdrop.

- **Add window dressing.** Windows are one of your shed's most important decorative elements, so highlight them any way you can. Always trim a window's exterior, adding color and dimension. Trim out the inset and windowsill on the inside too, and consider giving them a contrasting color.

2 | *The Architecture of a She Shed*

It might seem strange to use the term *architecture* when talking about sheds. After all, the basic shape of a shed is distilled down to the bare essentials: four walls, a floor, a door, and a roof. Yet architecture plays a significant role in making a she shed interesting and attractive.

Every building begins with some level of attention to architecture—decisions about length, width, ceiling height, and foundation type all fall into this category. However, architecture is also very much about the human being. (Who will be using this structure, and how?) The shed is no longer about keeping tools organized and covered; it is now a habitable structure meant to inspire creativity, reverie, camaraderie . . . or all the above!

A one-room structure can still bring a large variety of options and adapt itself to many styles and uses. Planning the architectural elements of your she shed can be deeply exciting.

Your Home's Architecture

Sometimes your home's architectural style will help shape your architectural plan for the she shed . . . but not always. In either case, it's a good idea to start planning your shed's architectural features by taking a good, hard look at the place in which you live.

What is it about your house that you like the most? What would you wish to improve upon? What are the elements that a realtor would play up in order to get potential buyers interested? These are some of the questions you might ask yourself as you walk around your home and really observe its shape, style, and decorative features.

Architecture often refers to a structure's style—Cape Cod, midcentury modern, cottage, ranch, and Craftsman styles come to mind. By breaking down those overarching design types, you can take a look at the smaller details that form a cohesive whole that speaks to you. Those details, which are often part of the building's construction that add to its form and/or function, are what this chapter is all about.

Massing

If you think of the shed as a miniature house, that means it's important to get a handle on the basics of massing and scale. Massing is simply the three-dimensional aspect of a home or other structure as you look at it. Our eyes take in not just the "face" of a house, but its entire footprint; how wide, how deep, and any kind of interesting protrusions (such as a porch) or voids (such as a courtyard or windows) all play into this concept.

Complex buildings such as cathedrals and castles can be broken down into parts, almost like a child's set of building blocks. Rectangles, cubes, domes, drums, and cylinders all come together to form the overall massing of a building.

For example, picture the shape of an old-fashioned gingerbread playhouse. Likely your vision contains a central pointed gable on the roof, which is trimmed with decorative carved bargeboards, divided-lite windows with window boxes underneath, and a front porch with railings and steps down to the garden. A faux chimney would be a nice touch too. Without thinking about it explicitly, your eye and brain immediately take in all these definitive "masses" to create a collective whole.

(Above) Fancy millwork, narrow double-hung windows, and a steeply peaked gable mark Sandy Foster's wonderful shed in the Catskills as carpenter gothic, or Victorian style. The front porch and lavish architectural details bring the structure closer to a small house than a traditional shed.

(Opposite) The simple lines of this shed are enhanced with elements that tie in the design with the house: fancy millwork, cream trim, brick pathways, and a complementary color palette. Note how the home's porch columns frame the she shed.

(Right) If you want a comfortable place to work, design a compact area of the shed with a built-in worksurface, cabinets, and sufficient knee space for your chair. The built-in desk shown here has a 26" depth, which takes up less than ⅓ the width of the 8' × 12' shed.

(Above) An important architectural principle asserts that many buildings do not literally reflect their purpose until important details have been added to them. This holds true for she sheds as well, because their beauty and originality emerge after the basic structure has been built.

Most sheds have extremely basic massing, their essence like a box with a single or dual-sloped roof. Still, massing is an important place to start, as it helps you determine the relationship between your shed's height, width, and depth. If you have a long width and a short height, your she shed might seem more like a chicken coop. Too tall and skinny, and it could be mistaken for a phone booth.

Scale

Working with scale and proportion is an important part of architectural design. Our brains and eyes just know when something is off or looks awkward, even if we can't explain why. The reason is usually because objects are not in proper proportion to each other, or they are poorly balanced.

In 1961, Disneyland unveiled a special grotto near Sleeping Beauty's Castle depicting Snow White and the Seven Dwarfs. The set of marble statues was a gift from an anonymous Italian carver . . . but there was a problem. Snow White was carved in the exact proportions of the tiny dwarves. Walt Disney nevertheless insisted on displaying them, and his clever design director John Hench figured out a solution. He placed Snow White high above her little friends, with a dramatic waterfall between them. Her height and distance made Snow White seem proportionate, especially with small-scale deer standing next to her.

This lesson is one to apply to your shed design as well. Your shed will very likely be small—smaller than anything you've considered hanging out in since you were 12 years old and still had a playhouse! Because you are more accustomed to furnishing and decorating a building that is at least 10 times the size of a shed, you're going to have to make some mental adjustments.

Working with scale will help you achieve a couple of style objectives. First, you will be able to make the most of your limited square footage by keeping things more compact. In a ship, every inch counts for fitting up comfortable living quarters and working space. The same holds true for a she shed. Consider every single part and furnishing for its size-to-benefits ratio: if that workbench takes up 25 percent of the room space, it better be worth it!

Last but not least, proper scale is more aesthetically pleasing. Our brains respond positively to balanced size and proportion, where one element doesn't overpower another.

Practicing Your Scale

Drawings such as the ones above were made using a CAD modeling program. Drawings are very useful in the beginning stages of a she shed plan and the program helps keep accurate scale, measurements, and two-dimensional perspective. However, this is at the advanced end of planning.

You can also hand draw using traditional tools, such as an architect's scale, T-square, metal ruler, and adjustable triangle.

By their nature, she shed owners do not like to be restrained by rules—this is a personal space and you can do whatever you please! Think of these tips as more of a framework that will help you get the look you want.

Draw to scale. Whether you are designing your shed from scratch or planning the interior of a kit shed, devise a ratio of feet to inches so that you can make a drawing. If the shed is 10 feet × 12 feet and you want your plan to fit on standard-size paper, use ½ inch for every 1 foot. Your shed floor plan on paper will then measure 5 inches × 6 inches. When drawing the elevation, or front view, of the shed, determine your wall height as well as its highest point (the apex) in feet, then convert to inches.

(Above) Examining the placement of clerestory windows on this modern shed style shows that while the windows have sufficient roof clearance along the front elevation, a slight adjustment might need to be made where the roof slopes down at the back.

(Below) Even this tiny she shed benefits from the principles of scale and good design. Note how the siding, trim, and window dimensions all conform to the overall size of the shed. Only the door is slightly overscale for ease of entry.

Utilizing limited space inside a she shed is aided by visualizing other small spaces, such as those on a ship. Here in her Mersea Island beach hut, Jane Ashmore has a cunning built-in bench seat that is long enough to sleep on. Made of solid wood and painted white, the bench seat opens to store beach toys and fold-up beach chairs.

Map both exterior and interior. Prepare a scaled drawing of the inside of your shed at the same time as the exterior. The two are intimately connected. Include furniture placement, built-ins, windows, and doors.

Consider built-ins and furnishings. When planning the interior, restraint is key. Worksurfaces that are built directly against the wall are ideal for taking up the least amount of space. If you are dead set on a center island or table, try to allow at least 18 inches of clearance around each side for ease of access.

Think like a landscape designer. The best she shed placement takes the entire backyard into consideration. Create a scaled map of the yard, noting hardscape, flowerbeds, driveway, etc. Draw the shed foundation and experiment with various angles, taking into consideration light exposure, setback from property lines, and the ability to open and close the front door (this is especially important in small yards). Think about the landscaping around the shed, especially the entryway.

The Golden Ratio

Since ancient times, builders have adhered to the principle of Phi, which is that any rectangle, when divided into a square and smaller rectangle, should maintain a 1:1.618 ratio. Phi is more than just proportional rectangles—it is a clean mathematical premise that, taken to its final shape as a Golden Spiral, dictates countless patterns in nature, from nautilus shell spirals to spiderwebs.

You can use the idea of the golden ratio to help you maintain symmetry, balance, and proportion within your shed design. The good news? Most of us adhere to this ratio without even knowing it.

- Windows and window placement: It's no coincidence that most double-hung windows come in sizes that conform to the golden ratio (12 × 20, 24 × 36, etc.). This works both vertically and horizontally (i.e., windows grouped in pleasing formations).
- Wall-to-roof ratio: The front elevation of a building often has a 1:1.618 ratio, the base being ⅔ taller than the gable portion.
- Shelf groupings: Along a wall you might have a larger square of clustered shelving or artwork, with the smaller rectangle staged as a reading area with chair and lamp.

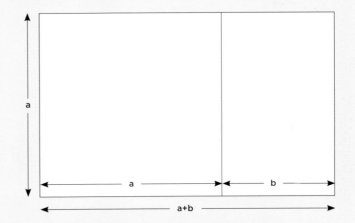

$$\frac{a}{b} = \frac{a+b}{a} = \mathbf{1.618}$$

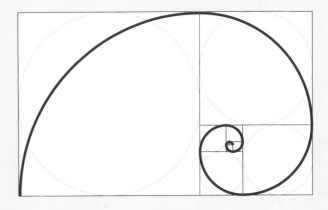

Exterior Enhancements

Once the structure of a shed is determined, architectural materials are selected that enhance its size and style. The process is both fun and somewhat daunting—there are a lot of different ways to go, and there is no right answer. Use your imagination, along with a generous portion of research, to create a she shed with beautiful exterior details.

You've probably already perused many sites and saved images of your favorites. Do you notice any patterns with your preferences? Look at your gallery and then make a list. Sooner or later your design process will start to filter out what you don't want and concentrate on what you do.

(*Above*) Traditional metal panels and galvanized steel are popular textural choices for she shed designers.

(*Opposite*) Simple cream paint allows this she shed's architectural features to come forward. A tasteful variety of shapes and patterns, including embossed tin panels and fish scale shingles, suggests an Old World garden conservatory.

Siding and Trim

The exterior walls of your she shed are a very important part of the architectural "message" you want to send. The material, profile (clapboard, board and batten, shingles, etc.), and of course color all make a huge impact on the look and style of your shed. Siding is also a place where you can exercise considerable creativity.

A very basic she shed that you might purchase at a home improvement store is usually clad in serviceable painted particleboard, vinyl, or metal. These siding options are fine for a structure that stores tools, but the stylish she shed owner might choose to go above and beyond, creating a custom shed built with different materials. Alternatively, you can modify the siding on a prefab shed by either cladding over it or changing its color.

Decorative exterior trim is siding's best friend. Trim can be as simple as framing windows in 3-inch wood molding, or more elaborate, with vertical and horizontal boards creating interesting patterns on the walls. Think about how important the cross trim on a barn door is for identifying what the building is for. You can capture that farmhouse, cottage, or even ultra-modern aesthetic by using trim designs in an effective way.

Materials

She sheds are composed of a wonderful array of materials. What you choose to use and the placement of these materials will contribute significantly to your structure's unique look and style. Metal, concrete, wood, and even synthetic components (such as polycarbonate panels) each offer properties of strength, protection, design appeal, or a combination of benefits. Get to know the different

This she shed is unabashedly eclectic, with several kinds of siding made of wood and metal, even burlap fabric (see right). Creative use of exterior material, pattern, and color results in a completely original look for your shed.

materials you can work with, and appreciate how they impart a certain look and feel to the structure, whether rustic, modern, romantic, or artistic. The unexpected quality of a she shed—using materials you may have never considered before—is one of the greatest joys in building one.

Wood

The foundation of nearly every she shed built, wood brings stability, strength, and style to the structure. Using new-growth, new-cut lumber offers a nice clean surface for painting and also avoids the warp, unevenness, and other flaws often found in scrap wood. Plywood and paint-grade wood are ideal canvases for adding color to both exterior and interior walls. You can even turn plain old plywood into something that looks more like mahogany or antique barn wood just by using some faux painting techniques. (See Chapter 3 for more detail on this.)

Another way to go is to use antique and salvaged wood material. There is nothing quite like the patina of pine or redwood that was milled in another time and place. She shed owners exult when they score a bundle of barn wood

Lumberyards and online classified sites are good places to find odd lots of wood with tons of character. It takes more work to prep and design, but the end results are usually worth it.

that was new at the turn of the last century. Stained, knot-holed, and gray with age, this type of wood has character, and it's ushered in a brand-new aesthetic called rustic, prairie, or farmhouse chic.

Wood pieces once considered throwaway are also becoming signature architectural features. I've met enterprising she shed owners who pulled wood from used pallets to clad the entire exterior surface of their sheds. Another couple built their modern-style shed using pieces of old scaffolding. Whether old or new, painted or stained, wood elements provide a feeling of warmth and permanence.

Metal

As versatile as it is practical, metal can be used in many creative ways on a she shed. Painted or not, fancy or a bit battered, metal embellishments include roofing materials, hardware, brackets, decorative appliqués, and outdoor furnishings.

Shed roofs are often covered with metal, because it is an effective barrier against moisture. Metal roofing panels are usually made from aluminum or steel, and in rare cases zinc or copper.

A real find: 100-year-old barn lumber that was headed to the scrap pile found a new home on the floor of Rachel Roe's art studio.

Working with Metal

Galvanized, corrugated, and stamped metal, once relegated to gritty agricultural, urban, and industrial structures, are now starring in wonderful she shed designs. Instead of a complete metal cladding, she sheds will often have panels of corrugated metal on the rooftop or punctuating walls. Here are some great ways to add interest to your she shed with metal.

A black metal grid surrounds the top of this modern cube-shaped artist studio. Along with its function as a trellis for the climbing ivy, the grid also creates a roof-like shape that gives architectural interest to the cube. Note how the metal window frames tie in nicely as well.

Metal panels are easy to find in home improvement stores and add a burnished touch to wood she sheds of all styles.

Architectural Trim

(Right) Use corrugated metal as a backsplash in a small bath, or behind your potting bench or work table. Design a metal wainscoting, or use it as a backing behind shelves.

Wall Panels

(Below) Try using panels of corrugated metal for exterior or interior walls. They look great when framed by wood trim.

Window Awnings and Window Boxes

(Above) Complement your windows with metal details. Use galvanized or zinc metal boxes instead of wood or plastic for planters under the windows. Window awnings are easy to make with some pretreated or painted wood pieces and a corrugated panel sized to fit over the window.

A standing seam roof is constructed with panels that are attached with continuous vertical metal ridges about ½ inch high; installed correctly, it will no doubt keep the rain out of your shed. Standing seam roofs are a bit more expensive than asphalt or shingles, but this option is worth considering both for its exceptional aesthetic and for the terrific melody the rain will make for you underneath.

Corrugated metal panels are experiencing a huge renaissance in the world of she sheds. These panels are made with galvanized steel that is then formed with grooves and ridges to increase its strength. Once used primarily over chicken coops and storage sheds, they are now seen far and wide on rustic and eclectic she sheds. You'll find them on rooftops, exterior siding, interior wall panels, window awnings, and fencing.

Masonry/Stone

Used since ancient times, masonry and stone have provided foundations, flooring, and walls for dwelling places that last for hundreds of years. Humans developed

Windows

One of the first things a child draws on a picture of her home are windows. Windows represent a pure marriage of form and function. They provide ventilation and light, views, and architectural beauty. When it comes to outbuildings, often windows are what distinguish a she shed from a tool shed. (Tools don't crave light and a view; women do.)

Give special consideration to the window or windows that grace the front of your shed. They are the eyes of your space and will look beautiful when embellished with fancy trim, vintage shutters, or bright painted window boxes. Feel free to push convention a bit, playing with asymmetrical placements or mixing modern and old-fashioned elements.

There are a few challenges involved with she sheds and windows, however. A small she shed, or one with a lower-than-average ceiling height, will have less space to devote to windows—especially if you plan to have built-in furnishings or a bed, or if you crave absolute privacy. A balanced approach and good planning are key. For example, a bank of narrow windows might be placed near the rafters to catch extra light while still allowing room for larger windows farther down.

Several small vintage windows are fitted together here in a unique way, resembling a quilt block. Don't be afraid to experiment with your shed's window design.

If you decide to build your she shed using a kit, pay careful attention to the size of the windows and the kind of glass that is included. It might be thinner or not as clear as you want. In this case, consider replacing the standard windows entirely with ones that are larger or even a different shape. Just make sure that the window framing is modified appropriately when you are building out your walls.

Carla Fisher's gardening shed is illuminated naturally, thanks to a roof made with polycarbonate panels. These panels are very strong, resisting chips and breaks more easily than glass.

extraordinary artisanal skills making different kinds of brick and laying them in intricate patterns. Stone surfaces are wonderfully attractive in all kinds of buildings, both commercial and residential. They can appear rustic—think river rock, granite, or slate—or very sophisticated, as in tumbled marble.

One interesting way to use stone is with gabion, the technique that encases small pieces of stone with a structure of heavy-gauge wire, formed to make fences or planters.

Manufactured Materials

Materials created by human enterprise include vital products, such as glass, plastics, resins, and even synthetic fabrics. Although we often gravitate toward the "all natural"

resources, we cannot build or decorate very well without the many options our modern world provides us.

What would windows be without glass, after all? Clear glass, leaded glass, and stained glass are the diamonds and gems of the she shed world. Consider also the retro/modern appeal of Seves glass block, perhaps used for accents.

Plastic and polycarbonate may sound sterile. However, these materials can be used for a variety of thoughtful purposes. Often in greenhouses, it's clear plastic that lets in plenty of light. The panels are often corrugated, but they also come flat with hollow cores to provide extra insulation. Gardeners and artists alike will appreciate the versatility of this material. Just take a look at the polycarbonate roof above.

Interior Elements

The architecture of your space extends to the design of the interior. In many respects, exterior elements influence the interior: roof structure, door and window placement, foundation shape, etc. Use your she shed's unique size, shape, and construction to enhance what it looks like on the inside.

Interior Walls and Dividers

Walls, even partial walls, help organize areas into specific uses. They are especially helpful if you want to contain storage and not-so-pretty necessities in some part of your shed. Depending on the size of your shed, you can design a permanent partition or simply make a nonstructural room divider that is easy to set up and remove.

If the square footage in your shed is high enough, usually at least 8 feet by 10 feet, you could create a segregated space using a half wall. A half wall (also called a knee wall or pony wall) is an interior wall that isn't load-bearing and is anywhere from 3 feet tall to just shy of the ceiling. It allows for light and airflow to come around and over the top, thereby maintaining a sense of openness.

Interior walls will take about 5 inches of floor space (in depth) after framing them out with 2 × 4 lumber. You can finish them with drywall, but also consider rustic wood or metal panels for added interest. If you have the room, consider giving your half wall more depth (at least 12 inches) so that it can hold cabinets or shelves for additional storage.

(Right) A half wall helps divide this busy she shed into two areas—the storage area remains somewhat hidden in the back.

(Opposite) The inside of your she shed should be designed for both comfort and style. Good window placement allows plenty of wall space for freestanding furnishings, even though this shed is only 6' × 9'.

Not enough space for an interior wall? Here's a simple trick to give yourself an extra "room" anyway. Vicki Sakioka wanted a small closet for her she shed that included a microwave and other necessities for overnight guests. She simply installed a couple of floor-length curtain panels a few feet away from the back wall. The drawn curtain keeps the closet out of sight.

Nooks, Crannies, and Alcoves

When a house is constructed, very often its framework and support system are completely hidden from view. Everything from the floorboards to the roof braces is sheathed in drywall or some other finishing material. While this is necessary for adequate insulation and energy efficiency, these coverings do eat up space.

Sheds do not necessarily require much in the way of finishes and often benefit from a more open feel. In this sense, they somewhat resemble Stick style architecture. This very popular nineteenth-century style featured decorative elements that represented the framework necessary for a built house; in effect, it celebrated the fundamentals of a structure. Inside a she shed, you can celebrate the exposed elements in much the same way—not only as decorative elements but also as very useful nooks and crannies. Here are some ideas:

(Top) Studs and braces inside a she shed create very natural framing for a variety of decorative elements. Use a contrasting paint or stain treatment, showcase display items, or emphasize hanging artwork within these spaces.

(Middle) Basic shelving comes with the territory—wall noggins are exposed in this shed design and are perfect to place items upon.

(Bottom) One of the best features of a she shed is the generous area underneath the roof. This rafter area is rarely covered with a drop ceiling, making it handy for a storage loft or simply to keep the shed feeling roomier.

- **Drop-down tabletop:** Tuck in a handy drop-down table or worksurface underneath or above a noggin (horizontal wood piece between wall studs). The noggin provides extra support.

- **Shelves:** Noggins make perfectly good natural shelves on their own; or you can extend them with a wider piece of wood supported by brackets.

- **Loft:** A spacious loft is the ultimate trade secret for tiny houses and she sheds. Lofts are platforms built in the triangular spaces created by open gables; they are the tiny attics of tiny structures and create very valuable space. Underneath the loft you have a bit of space to play with; this is a good place for a half wall.

- **Truss beams:** Exposed roof supports and cross beams add a lot to the visual interest of a she shed's interior. Use them to support light fixtures or for hanging plants. Enhance them with contrasting paint or stain.

Drop-Down Bar

This ingenious drop-down bar is the invention of Sean and Dana O'Brien of A Place to Grow/ Recycled Greenhouses, a designer and builder of she sheds in San Luis Obispo, California. Taking advantage of the area's cool Pacific breezes and giving a generous nod to the state's wine industry, the company's custom-designed she sheds that come with built-in bars are a great example of how to incorporate dual-purpose architectural elements. They make the perfect setting for an impromptu glass of wine with a friend or two.

The bar itself is actually a solid wood vintage door that is turned horizontally to be part of the shed's siding. Look for an old door that still has all its hardware intact and in good repair (doorknob with lockset, latchset, strike plate, and hinges). Your bar can go the entire length of your wall, or you can inset it within the wall framework, much like a window. When in use, the door/bar is pulled down and held in place with sturdy chain links. When not in use, you can push up the door and close it securely using the doorknob and strike plate.

Materials

- Sturdy door with all hardware
- Cleaning solution
- Sandpaper, 180 grit
- Rags
- Paint (optional, if repainting door)
- Chain link, 2/0 coil welded with a minimum 450 lb. working load-bearing capacity
- 4 eyebolts, $\frac{3}{8}$" × 4"
- 4 carabiners, $\frac{3}{16}$" quick link, rated at 450 lb.

Tools

- Work gloves
- Sander
- Paintbrush
- Painter's tape

  Note: *The above tools are optional—for use only if repainting the door.*

- Eye and ear protection
- Power drill
- Tape measure
- Jigsaw, chisel, or door latch installation kit
- Hammer
- Chain or bolt cutter
- Level

1 Sean and Dana started by preparing their door. They cleaned, sanded, and painted it to match the shed's look. At the same time, they removed the hardware with a power drill and set it aside in a cardboard box or bag.

2 They then turned their attention to the wall, framing the opening where they wanted to place the bar. They sized the measurement of the door positioned horizontally.

3 They attached one set of hinges to the bottom of the framed opening, aligning them to the hinge placement on the door.

4 At this point, it was time to replace the hinges and hardware back onto the door.

5 They installed a strike plate for the door latch at the top of the frame. They said it's possible to use a jigsaw, a chisel, or a door latch installation kit to chisel the wood frame so that the plate insets and is perfectly flush.

6 They brought the door to the frame and aligned the hinges together (it took at least two people to hold the door in place). Using a hammer, they set the hinge pin back into each hinge, making sure it was completely inserted. Then they brought the door up and closed it securely with the doorknob and strike plate.

7 For the chain, they measured the angle from the top of the bar frame to the outermost corner of door and cut the chain to fit. They double-checked to make sure the door rested perfectly horizontal for a level tabletop.

8 To finish up the project, they installed an eyebolt onto each of the door's outer corners. Then they installed an eyebolt into the upper portion of the frame of the inside wall on both sides in a structurally secure spot. Each eyebolt was next to those on the door when in the shut position. Then they attached the chains to the eyebolts using carabiners.

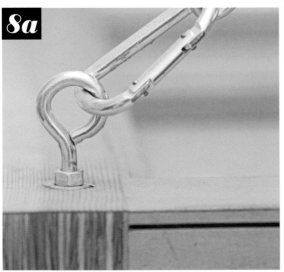

Materials

- Old bar cart
- Sandpaper
- Rags
- Primer
- Paint
- 2 × 4" × 8' pine boards for legs
- Wood glue
- ½" plywood for top of table
- Pocket hole jig screws
- 3½" × 8' pine boards for plank top
- Nails
- Wood conditioner
- Wood stain
- Stencils
- Painter's tape
- Newspaper
- Spray paint
- Clear satin finish

Tools

- Eye and ear protection
- Work gloves
- Power drill
- Sander
- Paintbrushes
- Tape measure
- Table saw
- Miter saw
- Pocket hole jig
- Clamps
- Square
- Level
- Nail gun

Built-In Sewing Table

This L-shaped work area is an ingenious combination of an old bar cart and a hand-built extension that is the same height and width as the cart. It fits snugly into one corner of a she shed; owner Nina McNamar uses it for her sewing projects. She made her own stencils, but you can take the store-bought route.

1 Nina's first order of business was removing any hardware from the bar cart with a drill. She also sanded down the cart to prepare it for painting.

2 After removing all the dust from the surface with a wet rag, Nina applied the primer and let it dry. After the cart had dried, she lightly sanded the primer. (Again, making sure to wipe any sanding dust from the cart.) She painted the cart aqua, applying the paint in the direction of the wood grain. Once the cart dried, she used coarse sandpaper to distress the edges.

3 When building the bar cart "L" extension, Nina needed it to be the same height as the bar cart. She determined the ideal length, then, using a miter saw, cut the 2 × 4 boards to the correct height for the legs. Then she cut the cross sections for the extension. She used a pocket hole jig to put pocket holes in the cross sections to connect the legs, gluing all the sections together and clamping securely. She used the square to make sure all the pieces were square.

4 Nina sanded the extension piece, then primed, painted, and distressed it the same way as the bar cart.

5 She cut down two 2 × 4 pieces to connect the bar cart and the extension. She used a pocket hole jig to connect all the pieces together.

6 At this point, Nina used a table saw to cut the plywood for the top of the table, though you can also ask your local hardware store to cut your pieces for you. Nina used a pocket hole jig to make pocket holes to connect the plywood L shape together, then she screwed the plywood down to the bar cart and the extension.

7 You'll need to plan how you want your planks to run for the top, then cut down your planks to desired lengths with your miter saw. Here, Nina used 12" planks, and the planks were started in the corner. She used wood glue and a nail gun to permanently position the planks. She worked from right corner to left, making sure the boards remained very straight. The top shown here started with a herringbone pattern in the corner, and then the planks were staggered in the next row.

8 Nina then stained the plank top. Once the top was finished, she sanded it until smooth, wiped off all the sawdust with a damp cloth, and applied a wood conditioner to the pine top. (This helps the stain go on smoothly.) Once dry, she wiped on aqua stain with a dry cloth and let it dry overnight.

9 To decorate the top, Nina used custom stencils, though stencils from the local craft store would work as well. She placed the stencils on the corners and taped them down with painter's tape, making sure to cover the worktop with newspaper to avoid overspray. She applied two very light coats of white spray paint, letting the coats dry in between. She then removed the stencil and all the tape and newspaper. She applied a clear satin finish to protect the top. (You can add decorative trim to the front and sides if desired.)

Decorative Window Frame

The interior frame of a window is sometimes neglected and appears rather plain. This project takes ordinary trim pieces and, with the help of a pretty pattern and a jigsaw, turns them into an attractive window frame. You'll need to feel comfortable using a few different power tools, but this is a good project on which to learn. At the end you'll have new skills and beautiful interior windows.

Materials

- 4" × 6' pine boards
- Paper
- Low-tack spray adhesive
- Sandpaper
- Rags
- Dark wood stain
- White paint
- Wood glue
- Pocket hole jig screws
- Nails

Tools

- Eye and ear protection
- Work gloves
- Tape measure
- Pencil
- Bandsaw or jigsaw
- Drill
- Sander
- Paintbrush
- Pocket hole jig
- Miter saw
- Clamps
- Nail gun
- Level

1

Top

Left

Right

Bottom

1 Nina started by measuring the window and, using the miter saw, cut four pieces of pine board for the window frame to the correct lengths.

2 She drew the shape that she wanted on paper (you can also print out a template that is the same size as the window pieces). A low-tack spray adhesive was used to position the template on the wood pieces.

2

Top *Bottom* *Left* *Right*

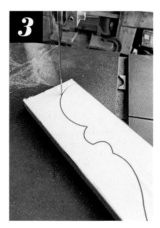

3

5a

5b

3 To cut out the pattern, Nina used a bandsaw or a jigsaw.

4 Nina sanded all the wood pieces with rough grit and then finely sanded them.

5 After removing any sawdust with a damp rag, Nina stained all the wood pieces with a dark wood stain and let them dry for several hours. Once completely dry, the boards were painted with white paint and allowed to dry completely. Once the paint dried, Nina used sandpaper to distress the wood.

6 Using a pocket hole jig, Nina made pocket holes on the backs of the wood pieces. She clamped down the wood pieces, placed wood glue on the ends, and screwed the frame together.

7 After everything was dry, Nina mounted the frame around the window using a nail gun; you can also use screws or a hammer and nails. (Use a level when you attach it to the wall.)

DIY Room Divider

Sheds are not always large enough to divide into rooms, yet designing some kind of partition is often valuable. Here is an idea for a completely portable room divider that can be made as large or as small as you want.

This project from Deborah Hayes calls for a set of two large wooden shutters that are joined with hinges. They can be positioned in any corner of a she shed and become decorative shields for boxes and projects that are stored behind them. Each of the slats on the shutters is embellished with ruffled fabric or lace.

Materials

- 2 shutters, each approximately 18″ wide × 6′ tall
- Cleaning solution
- Sandpaper
- Rags
- Paint (if repainting shutters)
- Fabric, lace, or wide ribbon
- Thread
- 2 hinges

Tools

- Eye and ear protection
- Work gloves
- Paintbrush (if repainting shutters)
- Power drill or Phillips screwdriver
- Tape measure
- Scissors or rotary cutter and self-healing mat
- Sewing machine or needle
- Hot glue gun

1 Deborah started by preparing the shutters. She used a cleaning solution to remove dust and dirt, then sanded lightly and removed the dust with damp rags. This is the time to repaint your shutters if necessary. (Remove any unwanted hardware as well with a drill or screwdriver.)

2 Deborah counted the slats and measured their width and length. Then she multiplied the total number of slats by their length: 80 slats with a 14″ length equaled 1,120″.

3 Fabric, lace, and ribbon are sold by the yard, so in the case of 80 slats with a 14″ length, she needed about 31 yards of fabric (1,120 divided by 36″).

4 For fabric, Deborah cut 3″-wide strips. Thus, one yard of 45″-wide fabric will yield about 15 ruffles if it's cut lengthwise. **Tip:** For ungathered strips (fabric, lace, or ribbon), cut at least 1.5 to 2 times the slat length. For pre-gathered strips, cut to fit the slat length.

5 To make the ruffles, you can use a machine or sew by hand. To gather by machine: Use a wide basting stitch about ⅜″ from the top of the fabric. Pull thread ends gently on both sides until fabric is evenly gathered and the correct length; secure with knots. For thicker fabrics, zigzag stitch over a long piece of button thread. Gently pull thread from either side to evenly gather the fabric. Secure each end with knots. To gather by hand: Hand baste about ⅜″ from the top of the fabric. Secure one end and pull the thread to gather it to the desired length; knot both ends.

Make It Easy

- Use pre-ruffled ribbon and lace so that you don't have to machine- or hand-gather your fabric. (You will also require less yardage!)
- If your fabric is very lightweight, then a high-tack double-sided tape can be substituted for hot glue.
- Found the perfect ribbon but it's too wide? Fold over one edge and then gather it for a fuller ruffled look.

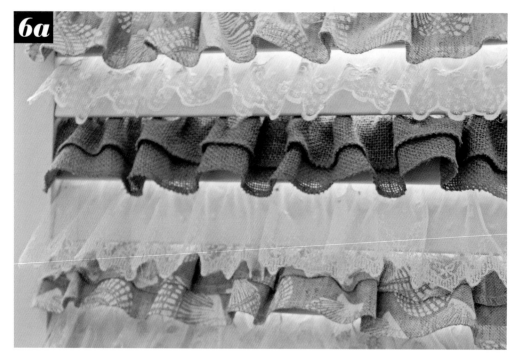

6 Deborah arranged the gathered strips in the desired pattern. Ruffled bottoms of each strip face toward the front.

7 With a glue gun, Deborah placed a dot of glue on one end of the first slat and attached the gathered strip. She continued by adding a light line of glue along the rest of the slat and pressing the fabric firmly. This process was repeated with all the remaining slats.

8 With the decoration finished, she then attached hinges using a power drill.

Both the little girl and the grown woman inside of us inform our decisions about the color of our she sheds. With a cottage style like mine, the palette choices are wide and flexible. Wanting color without verging on the carnival, my palette includes Sunrise Dahlia, a creamy yellow, for the main color, punctuated by a periwinkle door created by mixing cream with a deep blue.

3 | *What Color Is Your She Shed?*

It's a fun day when you are ready to select the color for your she shed. If you're lucky, you might have several areas where color is going to have a starring role. Your plan should include exterior walls, interior walls, window trim, roof trim, floors, the door—they are all waiting for you to put your own personal color style onto a brush and start painting away.

At least that's the way I see it! I realize, though, that choosing paint colors is a dreaded chore for some. As you face walls of paint chips at the paint store, they look so pretty and enticing—how are you going to narrow the thousands down to one hundred, let alone to one or two? What if it's too yellow or too bright?

Whether you are the type who embraces or avoids the challenge of paint selection, remember that the outcome is going to be one gorgeous she shed, done exactly the way you want it. Invest some time in understanding color a little better and experimenting, and it will really pay off.

Understanding Color: Hues, Tints, Tones & Shades

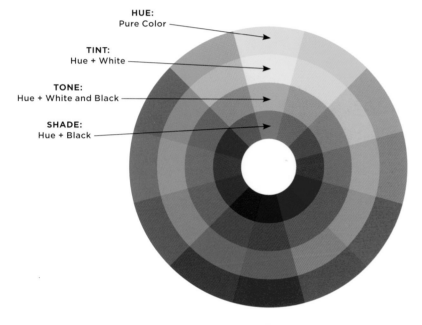

HUE:
Pure Color

TINT:
Hue + White

TONE:
Hue + White and Black

SHADE:
Hue + Black

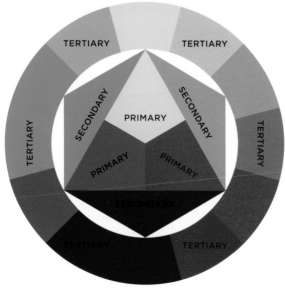

The color spectrum is vast, but it has a pleasing organization that can help you make wise decisions about your palette. It all starts with the three primary colors we all know from kindergarten: red, yellow, and blue. In their pure forms, they are true standalone colors and cannot be produced by mixing any other colors. Primary colors are very literal and bright, great for kids' playgrounds and toys but usually too loud for she sheds.

From these three primary colors, secondary colors are born. Blending red and blue makes purple; blending yellow and red makes orange; and blending blue and yellow makes green. Tertiary colors are created by mixing primary and secondary colors together, as well as black and white pigments. This is when you begin to see the subtle but important variations of a single color—hot pink is very different from rose pink, which is different from ballet slipper pink.

Adding white and black to the spectrum provides immense variety. Tints are colors to which white has been added; shades are colors darkened with black. Hue is a term that identifies a color by its predominant wavelength, so if you are trying to get a golden peach color you might ask for something with an orange hue. What is important for you is to find colors that are attractive in your landscape; that complement each other as exterior, interior, trim, and door colors; and that please your own personal taste.

Artist Ali Ferguson chose to paint both the walls and the ceiling of her shed the same vivid blue. This monochromatic scheme is set off by the ceiling's crossbeams, which are painted in a contrasting color.

Color Selection Tips

This might be the very first time you've been in charge of selecting the color for your space. A house is often painted before it's purchased, and in some communities only a limited palette of shades is allowed in order to keep things looking consistent. It's a very exciting responsibility, so keep it fun. Here are some easy ways to do this.

Process of Elimination

Start with the negative: decide which colors you *do not* want. By filtering out the colors you dislike, that would not complement the design of the shed, or that are jarring with the landscape, you end up with a much more manageable selection of colors.

Buy Sample Sizes

More and more paint manufacturers and home improvement stores offer small containers of paint so you can test before you invest. Sample sizes are about 8 ounces and priced below $5, which means you can test 10 colors for the cost of a single gallon.

Have a Paint Party!

Evaluating paint by committee, if it's a committee of people whose company and taste you admire, is a great way to help you select your color. Throw a paint testing party, inviting friends and neighbors to paint a swatch and give their two cents on the results. If you're lucky, they might come back to help with the final paint job. (For more on this idea, see page 65.)

Change Happens

Just as you repaint your home's interior from time to time to freshen up a room or reflect a new decorating style, you can do the same for your shed. Today's pastel shade might reflect a restful need. Tomorrow you might be exploring the artist within, and vivid, pigment-rich colors may be the order of the day. Paint is inexpensive and easy to redo, so you'll never be stuck.

Narrowing It Down

One way to get started on your color journey is by evaluating color according to your shed's function and architectural design. Although there are nearly infinite possibilities for shed color, there are going to be some colors and color combinations that will just "feel right" over the rest. Historic precedent has formed alliances between certain color palettes and the structure's use:

Barn	=	Brown, Red, White, Yellow
Poolhouse/Cabana	=	Blue, White
Cabin	=	Natural wood, Neutrals

Think about the landscape style you have (or want to have). Is your ideal backyard sleek and suburban, or does it have a more ruffled and wild look? Sleek and suburban colors might include a range of dark grays, dark blues, or sand/stone shades. The untamed rural yard can range widely, from traditional outbuilding colors (brown, red, white, yellow) to gray-greens or even a bright pop of cerulean blue.

Another thing to consider is whether to blend or go bold. Blending in with your backyard surroundings means selecting a color palette that makes the she shed recede a little bit into the foliage. Another way to blend is by matching your she shed to the main house. This can look especially nice if the property is small and the architectural styles are similar.

Rebecca Lynne Spencer didn't want to completely restore her old shed but wanted to make it appealing and prevent it from falling down. She shored up the structure and painted it a bright blue, added a few decorative elements, and enhanced the landscape surrounding it. The improvement is striking.

The Exterior Palette

Sheds, like colors, hold infinite possibilities, but sometimes it's necessary to filter infinity down a bit. To do this, I'm going to sort she sheds into five main categories: eclectic, green, modern, romantic, and rustic. Each design category reflects architectural type, what the shed is used for, and gives at least a nod to color palettes that are often associated with them. Consider these groupings for the exterior, interior, and trim color palettes you are striving for or simply use them as a springboard while searching out your own.

Eclectic. The artsy, the bohemian, the anything-goes-and-take-no-prisoners woman looks to a she shed that is funky and colorful. This is the place where blending and matching are not on the invite list. Nevertheless, it all just seems to work, whether it's a bright pop of lemon yellow, a warm cinnamon, or even a "painted lady" combination of purple, green, and yellow.

Garden/Green. Using your she shed as a place to help you keep your garden thriving truly makes it part of the natural landscape. Colors found in nature are nice choices, particularly those in the green, brown, and rose families. Love wisteria or lilacs? Think about a shed color that will set them off, such as cream or pale yellow. However, don't forget about the rich color of weathered wood, which happens to pair beautifully with foliage of any hue.

Modern/Zen. The modernist movement stems from a rejection of the past. In art it meant moving into abstract shapes and color that defied visual reality, which up until then was how artists would usually paint. Modern style is about embracing science, human advancement, and the future. Zen aligns with the principles of modern style in a couple of ways—it celebrates the beauty of function and simplicity, comfort and purpose. A sense of severe beauty, or sometimes really bold color, will highlight the modern shed in an astonishingly beautiful way.

Romantic/Shabby. In its infancy, the shabby chic style emphasized the beauty of leaving things alone in all their faded, chipped glory. Think whitewashed barn planks, gentle pastels, and painted-over metal bed frames paired with clean, soft canvas sofa slipcovers, chandeliers, and pillows. Since then, the look has matured to embrace deeper colors and stained wood. Hues within the turquoise, lavender, and rose palette are always good bets for a feminine, romantic feel.

Rustic. The rustic look is a priceless gift because it makes just about any rundown, scrappy little shed a diamond in the rough. Choose rustic for a cozy, bohemian place that exudes charm where it may lack refinement. One path is to embrace the natural patina of weathered wood, perhaps staining it so that the grain shows through. Another option is incorporating colors associated with farming and the rural life, such as deep reds, cheery yellows, and good-for-everything antique whites.

Many people are drawn to fanciful gingerbread millwork and trim such as the ornamentation on Shirley Gibson's art studio. Refusing any restraint, Shirley's love of color is played out on just about every kind of millwork known to man. The result is both artful and childlike.

Paint Primer

Here are a few quick tips to help you paint like a pro.

- **Always prime before painting.** Priming the surface before painting is well worth the effort. A good layer of primer neutralizes the surface so your paint color comes out better starting with the first coat. It also helps the paint adhere better and last longer.
- **Use the proper paint formulation.** There are important differences between exterior and interior paint. Exterior paint contains ingredients that help it withstand sun and moisture exposure. Interior paint is more delicate and will usually contain fewer or no VOCs (volatile organic compounds) to reduce emissions.
- **Add color to your primer.** Here's a tip from a custom paint manufacturer: add some of your paint color to the primer before application. The tinted primer helps retain the true shade of your paint and aids in full coverage of the wood beneath.

Interior Palettes

Besides adding visual interest, paint and stain serve other useful purposes. They protect the surfaces of your walls from dirt and moisture, and they also dramatically affect light, especially for interiors. The lighter your paint color, the more it will reflect light and reduce shadow.

This is the primary reason that many, many she sheds have white, cream, or light gray walls. With the average shed measuring less than 120 square feet, a light-painted surface is going to work wonders for conveying a more spacious feel.

Light and neutral is not the only way to go, however. Wall color has proven psychological benefits—an entire industry has been built around prescribing color for its therapeutic and health-boosting properties. For your shed, it always boils down to the default rule: do what you want. Here are a few ideas to get you going.

Lighter version of the exterior. Add white to your exterior color and get a softer version for the interior walls.

Blend the two with a ratio that you'll remember (i.e., ¼ cup at a time), then stir and test between each addition. When you get to the shade you want, note the amount of white paint added just in case you need to blend again.

Highlighting a furniture piece. Perhaps you are fortunate enough to have an heirloom area rug you want to put in the shed. Pick out one of the rug's accent colors and use that on the walls. This will create a pleasing connection between wall and floor.

Accent wall. Accent walls, where one wall is painted a vivid color against a more neutral color on the rest, are tailor made for she sheds. You get added color interest while at the same time allowing light to reflect off the lighter surfaces.

Trim. Do not underestimate the power of trim color. Try for a contrasting yet complementary paint that enhances your base color. There are lots of ways to go, but again it mostly boils down to personal preference. Because I admire Craftsman and Victorian architecture, I gravitate to lively palettes that bring the door and trim to life with

The interior of my shed is a considerably lightened version of my door color. Adding cream or white in measurable portions to a saturated color like my original Twilight blue created versions of blue and blue-purple that were exactly what I wanted. Don't hesitate to mix your own colors, but make sure you keep track of the recipes.

a secondary or even a tertiary color. That's not to say that a she shed can't be painted completely in one color (trim, door, and all).

Use trim color to highlight architectural elements (window frames, eaves), millwork (porch posts, baseboards), or focal points (decorative medallions).

To figure out a good trim color, refer to the color wheel and the palette that corresponds to your she shed type. Consider your home's color palette too—picking up the body color as your shed's trim color can be a nice way to tie the two together.

Color by Committee: The Paint Party

It can be lonely choosing color. That's why throwing a paint testing party might be the thing to get you off the fence, color-wise. Invite your neighbors and friends to help you paint a selection of colors on your shed walls and provide feedback. Keep it short, fun, and festive. Here are a few steps to make it happen.

1. Send out invites and be specific on timeframe. Keep it to no more than an hour out of respect for your friends' busy lives.
2. Refreshments are not optional. Have tasty brunch food and maybe a tray of Bloody Marys and orange juice to keep everyone happy.
3. Have everything organized before the guests arrive. Lay out paints and fresh brushes and make sure there is plenty of siding ready for the testing to take place.
4. Ask each attendee to paint one or two swatches on the siding. When that is done, give everyone an evaluation form with the colors listed. Ask each person to select her favorite and explain her choice.

When the party is over, calculate and analyze the results. Hopefully your guests will provide written comments, but consider the conversations you had as well. Chances are your friends were helpful, as they at least pointed out considerations you hadn't thought of before.

(Above) Invite your friends and neighbors to help you decide what color to paint your she shed! It's fun and gives you valuable objective feedback.

(Below) I learned a lot from my own paint party. If you've already narrowed down your finalist colors, then your friends and neighbors can help you come up with a winner.

Decorative Paint Techniques

Decorative painting is all about using color in unique ways to achieve special effects. You've no doubt seen cool murals or script lettering on kitchen walls, and perhaps you've tried your hand at stenciling a design somewhere in your home. If you enjoy experimenting with paint techniques, you are in the right place. A she shed is for playing. Consider it a lab for creativity, where you can try something new and see how it looks . . . then try again.

Stenciling is one of the easiest ways to achieve a pretty decorative effect. Stenciling refers to isolating areas for coloring by covering the remainder of the area, usually with a sheet of acetate. You might have a single stencil layer or several layers that are laid over the same spot to create a design with multiple colors. You can use a stencil design to cover all of your walls or just a single accent wall.

The technique of *faux bois* ("false wood") was practiced liberally in the Victorian era. Interior wood elements (such as doors, baseboards, and stairways) made of inexpensive fir were skillfully painted using layers of color and glaze to look very much like mahogany, quarter-sawn oak, or walnut grain. Found an old solid wood door already painted in an ugly gray? *Faux bois* returns it to its natural wood beauty, at least in appearance. You'll find many tutorials and books on the subject, and the results are delightful for wood grain lovers everywhere.

Stains and Washes

While paint may be top of mind when adding color to your shed, stain is also very worthy of consideration. A stain is a thin, oil- or water-based liquid carrying pigments and colorants. When applied to wood or another porous surface, it instantly stains it. Stain, often along with a final sealer, protects the wood while allowing the wood's natural color and grain to show through. Stains are either semitransparent or opaque. A semitransparent stain gives a fine patina of color while the wood's markings stay visible. An opaque stain, on the other hand, almost (but not quite) eliminates them.

You can achieve some spectacular results using stain. While most people think of stains as a palette of wood tones that simply enhance wood's natural color, that's only half the story. In fact, stains come in a rainbow of colors—azure blue, barn red, Bordeaux, green, gray, and more.

Painted wood floors can be traced back hundreds of years. In early American homes, clever artisans painted plain pine floors to look like marble or tile. Artist Shirley Gibson enhanced her own plain wood floors with an enchanting diamond pattern featuring negative-space cats on a black background.

Here are some ideas for using stain in the she shed:

- Know how to get a wonderful aged patina onto brand-new boards straight from the lumberyard? Use a gray-toned stain, rub it into the wood, and then quickly wipe. This finish makes the wood appear to have been weathered over time without the wear and tear.

- Use a combination of paints and stains for walls. Consider a stain color that complements your paint color. Use it on alternating planks or perhaps as a trim color. See page 71 for a step-by-step project using this technique.

- Use stain instead of paint to make stenciled designs on your wood walls or floor. You can even create a negative-space design by masking the design itself and using stain around it.

Whitewashing

In earlier times, people used a mixture of hydrated lime, salt, and water to make homemade paint. The result was a thin white coating that would provide weather protection to wood fences, barn siding, and other unpainted surfaces. The lime also acted as a rot and insect deterrent.

If you are a lover of natural wood but want a little light and softness in your space, you may consider the modern version of whitewashing for your she shed. Whitewashing today is simply a technique of diluting white or cream paint with water so that it is translucent. The mixture goes on easily with a roller and is then rubbed with a rag. The best thing about whitewash is that it lets the natural grain of the wood show through. It also economizes on paint, as a single quart of paint will very likely get the whole inside of a she shed looking great. If you use whitewash on the exterior, finish with a couple of coats of sealer to protect the wood.

Colorwash

Take the whitewash concept and use a color instead: *voilà*, you have colorwash! Combining a painted surface with the look of natural wood, you now have a pretty tint thrown in. Colorwash has a similar look to a stain, but it's a great

Whitewashing produces a gentle, faded effect that is very appealing. Use it to rehab old stained wood or lighten a dark room. The look is compatible with shabby chic/romantic and French-style interiors.

technique because it allows you to get more use out of all those partially used cans of paint in the garage.

Colorwash can be a glaze, where you add a bit of paint to water and then brush it on a surface. Another way to do this is to dry brush the paint color of choice onto the wood, then wipe it with a wet rag.

Chalked Paint Nightstand Makeover

Some of your colorful projects within the shed might include painting or repainting furniture. This nightstand is a great size for a small room, providing a surface for working or reading as well as a useful storage drawer. Rebecca Ittner used chalked paint to give it a soft luminescence. Chalked paint is particularly appealing in that it hides imperfections very well, often with a single coat.

Materials

- Sandpaper, medium and fine grit
- Phosphate-free pre-paint cleaner (optional)
- Annie Sloan's Chalk Paint or similar (Rebecca used pink and white)
- White or colorfast rags
- Top coat/sealer for chalked paint

Tools

- Eye and ear protection
- Latex or vinyl gloves
- Tarp
- Screwdriver
- Large flat paintbrush
- 2 medium or large round paintbrushes
- 2 small flat paintbrushes
- Paint stirrers
- Plastic container

Note: If your item is very old or dirty, you will first need to use a pre-paint cleaner. Doing so will remove oils and residues that could prevent paint from adhering to the surface of the nightstand. Follow the manufacturer's directions, and wear gloves, a face mask, and eye protection.

1 Rebecca covered her worksurface with a tarp. She removed the drawer from the nightstand, using a screwdriver to remove the drawer handle, and set it aside. She sanded all the uneven areas, including rough edges, dusting afterward with a large flat paintbrush.

2 Using the round paintbrush and white chalked paint, Rebecca covered the entire piece, including the drawer front. She used the bristle end of the brush to push paint into any cracks or carved areas and used the small flat brush along the edges of the table and drawer. (The drawer handle can be painted too, if desired.) After the paint dried, she applied a second coat of white chalked paint and allowed it to dry.

3 Next came the pink chalked paint; Rebecca stirred the paint thoroughly, poured some of the paint into a plastic container, and added a few drops of water until the paint was thin but not watery. She then applied the pink paint as a wash over the white paint on the table. (The drawer was left white.) She moved slowly and used a rag to adjust the thickness and spread the paint, allowing some of the white to show through. When done, she let the paint dry completely.

4 Using a medium-grit sandpaper, Rebecca lightly distressed the table and drawer front, allowing areas of wood to show. Then she used the fine-grit sandpaper to let white areas show through.

5 Rebecca applied a top coat/sealer to the table and drawer front, following the manufacturer's directions, and allowed it to dry completely.

6 Finally, she attached the drawer handle and inserted the drawer back into the nightstand.

Stained and Painted Siding

A fanciful alternative to walls painted all one color, this variegated horizontal siding is the creative work of she shed owner Nina McNamar. Using various painting techniques such as dry brushing and ombre, Nina gave ordinary plywood planks a highly artistic look. You can also get this look with salvaged siding of all types. This is a project even those with beginner painting skills can do.

Materials

- 4' × 8' sheets of ¼" plywood
- Sandpaper
- Aqua paint
- White paint
- Weathered gray stain
- Light wood-colored stain
- Rags
- Nails

Tools

- Eye and ear protection
- Work gloves
- Table saw
- Sander
- Paintbrushes
- Level
- Nickels (for spacing the planks)
- Compressor
- Nail gun
- Hammer
- Miter saw

1 Nina had her local hardware store cut down the 4' × 8' sheets of plywood to 4' × 4' sheets for easy handling. She then used a table saw to cut down the sheets into planks to get an even number of planks with minimal waste. Nina sanded all the planks both front and back to knock off the rough edges.

2 Nina painted and stained all the planks in the desired colors. No matter your color scheme, it's best to vary the design by painting some of the planks, staining some, and then adding dry-brush effects to some once they are dry. Use old rags for additional paint effects on the planks.

3 Once the planks were completely dry, Nina distressed them either by hand with sandpaper or with a hand sander. Some of her planks were heavily distressed and some were passed over completely. She also did some ombre effects by painting one shade of color and then feathering in a darker or lighter version with a paintbrush.

4 Figure out a pattern you would like your planks to run in. You could run your planks vertically, horizontally, or even in a diagonal pattern. Nina chose horizontal planks, starting from the bottom and working her way up. She then cut them into various lengths using the miter saw.

5 She lined up her planks starting at the bottom and working up. Nina used a level to ensure the boards were straight, and she placed nickels between the boards for even spacing. Use a compressor and nail gun to attach the planks if possible; otherwise, use a hammer and nails. Nail your boards one at a time in the desired pattern.

Antiqued Siding

You'll be surprised (in a good way) by how much color and character can be added to plain wood. You'll soon see why Sabrina Contreras likes using a dry-brush technique on her wood, using either flat paint, oil-enriched cabinet enamel, or even tinted polyurethane on its own. The color latches onto the wood in streaks and patches, creating an effortless antiqued look.

Materials

- New cedar or Douglas fir pallet wood
- Flat paint, cabinet enamel, or tinted polyurethane in black, gray, or cream
- Clear polyurethane

Tools

- Eye and ear protection
- Latex gloves
- Paintbrushes

Antiquing Wood

Here are a few other ways to antique your wood:

- Use a tinted polyurethane directly on new wood for a rustic look. You can purchase tinted polyurethane in a variety of colors or make your own using universal color pigments.
- Oil-enriched cabinet enamel creates a lovely stain-like finish that is durable and smooth looking. It also cleans up with water.

The floor boards get a refined treatment with two strokes: light paint combined with enamel, and a dark gray cabinet enamel.

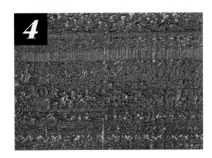

1 Sabrina prepped her wood by brushing it clean of dust particles. She dipped a paintbrush into flat paint, wiping off excess on the paint jar. She then brushed the wood in the direction of the grain with light, consistent strokes.

2 After the coat dried, Sabrina turned the brush and used the narrow edge to add uneven marks, and then let it dry.

3 She continued with a few more strokes, with the broad edge of the brush, until she got the distressed look she wanted.

4 After the final layer was dry, she brushed the wood with three coats of clear polyurethane for outdoor protection.

Faux-Painted "Brick" Floor

Carla Fisher's kit shed came with a thick plywood floor base. It was practical for a potting shed, but Carla wanted something more than just a coat of paint. She decided to go with a faux-painting technique to create a gray brick pattern, substituting opaque wood stain for paint. The process has a few steps and a bit of drying time, but is certainly doable, even for novice painters. It is remarkable to see how sponging on the various colors achieves the textured effect of masonry.

Materials

- Opaque wood stain: gray (grout), medium gray (bricks), dark gray (shadow), contrasting gray (similar to brick color), and white (highlight)
- Painter's tape, 1″ wide

Tools

- Eye protection
- Work gloves
- Kitchen sponges
- Sponge brush

Tip: Press the tape down firmly so the color doesn't seep through. To create bricks with "broken" corners, cover the corners with tape.

1 Carla painted the entire plywood floor with her "grout" stain color and let it dry.

2 Using painter's tape, she then created a brick pattern. Carla used a kitchen sponge as a guide but made the bricks slightly smaller. She alternated each course (line) of bricks to create a pleasing design.

3 Carla then painted the entire floor again with the background brick color (medium gray) and let it dry.

4 Using a sponge brush, Carla applied three colors to the sponge in a haphazard pattern: dark gray, contrasting gray, and white.

5a

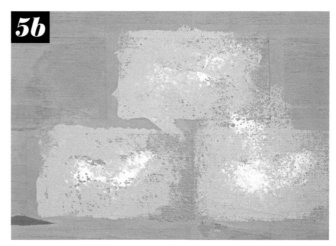

5b

6

5 She pressed the sponge down onto the taped rectangles, continuing until the entire floor was painted. She used various stamp positions and repeated stamps here and there so that every brick appeared slightly different.

6 When the floor was completely dry, Carla removed the tape.

4 | *Interior Design: Shed Style Defined*

Interiors in she sheds can be just as magical as the memory of a favorite childhood tree house or playhouse—only this time all grown up. Many of the effective design principles used in home interiors are relevant for the shed as well, including scale, flow, and cohesion. Yet with these considerations comes a certain freedom because this is, after all, your shed.

The interior style of a shed often corresponds to its exterior—if the shed is built in the cottage or traditional style, then chances are its furnishings and decorative elements inside will be too. But this isn't always the case, as seen in perhaps a very old shed that has been restored and dressed with an ultra-modern interior. You can achieve a dramatic and attractive contrast, perhaps speaking to two sides of your own personality.

Jane Ashmore's beach hut, part of the Little Beach Hut Company, is designed with making memories in mind. Everything from the sturdy whitewashed vinyl flooring to the color scheme aligns with a relaxed seaside vibe. Note also the clever use of wall space for shelves, cabinets, and built-in benches.

So, where to begin? One place to start is with color, selecting your palette and designing around that. A very striking technique might be a monochromatic interior (such as cream or pale blue) brightened with spots of color, or you can cozy it up with layer upon layer of rich, deep colors in your textiles and finishes. Another way to go is from the ground up: let your flooring and perhaps a stunning area rug define the room and furnishings. A third option for the organized and practical among us is to let form follow function. Create your necessary storage and organization and let the artistry be informed from there. Use the approach that works best for your own distinct style; the pages ahead touch on the special areas of a shed that will need your attention.

Designing a Small Space

Most she sheds run on the small side compared to a house, which means making the most of every inch. In the midst of all the fun stuff—flooring, furnishing, shelving, and decorative touches—make sure you have enough room to step in! If it's too crammed with furniture and knickknacks, you won't enjoy it or use it as much.

Going back to the "what am I using it for" question will help you with a plan. A gardening shed must have space for managing plants, storing tools, and planning next season's garden. A reading shed needs a comfortable chair, bookshelves, and good light. The artist, besides needing plenty of natural light, will want an open floor plan that includes a work table and space to move around from project to project with a portable supply caddy in tow.

Start with a simple space plan on paper, and draw the dimensions of the shed floor—1 inch for every foot is a typical ratio. Then consider the larger pieces you must have, and position them where they fit best. Windows are wonderful, but they use up wall space where a tall storage cabinet might go. It's best to know what you are going to want against your walls, such as built-in furniture, and size the windows accordingly.

As noted in Chapter 2, built-ins are great additions to shed design because they are very efficient in terms of their footprint. Consider building in a work table against one wall or in an L shape, with cabinets or open shelving underneath as well as space for a chair. Other built-ins to consider are corner shelves, upper wall cubbies, shelves, and lofts. If there is room on the outside, you can even consider adding a "built-out"—a neat little closet behind or on the side of your shed.

This simple work table fits snugly under the shed window, which also provides good natural light for sewing projects.

Interior designer Alexis King chose a self-healing tackable wall covering for three of her four walls. This is handy for pinning up fabric samples and color swatches while she works.

Tiny Feng Shui Tips

Feng shui is the arrangement of a structure to harmonize with the energy that inhabits it. It may sound "out there," but feng shui is actually a remarkable tool that makes an interior feel and flow better. There are a few feng shui principles that can really enhance your design efforts. Here are three tips for the she shed:

- **Control clutter.** It's not easy, because your she shed houses items from two sources—decoration and utility. Somehow you need to make space for the things you'll need for gardening, painting, or crafting. You will need to make your storage and organization solutions as attractive as possible.

- **Watch the door.** Try to position your workspace or reading nook so that you are facing the door, ideally from the side. It isn't good *ch'i* (energy) to turn your back on the door or other people. If you have a built-in workspace and face the wall,

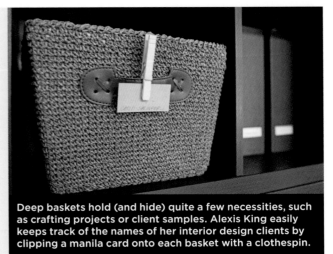

Deep baskets hold (and hide) quite a few necessities, such as crafting projects or client samples. Alexis King easily keeps track of the names of her interior design clients by clipping a manila card onto each basket with a clothespin.

consider adding a pretty mirror so that you can still see in your prosperity direction.

- **Consider your light sources.** Good, natural light is a must in the she shed. Using light and creamy colors helps lighten the room. However, keep in mind that bright, rich color is considered a positive light and energy source too.

Instead of eating up precious space inside the she shed, this nice-sized lean-to storage closet was added to the back of Rachel Roe's shed.

What to Put Underfoot

There is something fundamentally nurturing about the floor we walk on. Perhaps it is because as babies we felt every bump and knew every loose fiber in the carpet as we slowly crawled our way across the room. That floor was home base! A floor is firm and steady under the feet, supporting your body weight as you go about your daily life. A good floor in your she shed is something that you'll enjoy for many years to come.

Flooring comes in a wide variety of materials, textures, and colors and is usually one of the earliest decisions made in your she shed design. Why? Because very often the type of foundation you have affects your flooring choices.

If you have a dry, level area in the yard that has good drainage, then you might opt for a concrete foundation (also called a slab foundation). Ideal flooring for concrete would be vinyl, tile, or even the cement itself. Wood floors can be installed on top of concrete, but there is a risk of

moisture seeping in and causing the wood to warp. To avoid this, you should frame your floor just above the concrete and install it on wood supports.

Consider masonry and fine gravel as well, especially if you plan to make your she shed a place for gardening. She sheds made with as many natural materials as possible are very attractive and integrate beautifully with the landscape.

Raised foundations, in which the shed is supported above ground level on piers, offer a variety of flooring options, from wood to vinyl to tile. Brick floors are somewhat heavy and aren't recommended on a raised foundation.

To narrow it down, consider your overall style, the use (or abuse) your floor will likely endure, the level of difficulty to install, and, of course, your budget. The good news regarding budget is that most shed floors are not very large, and thus you don't have to buy a lot of product.

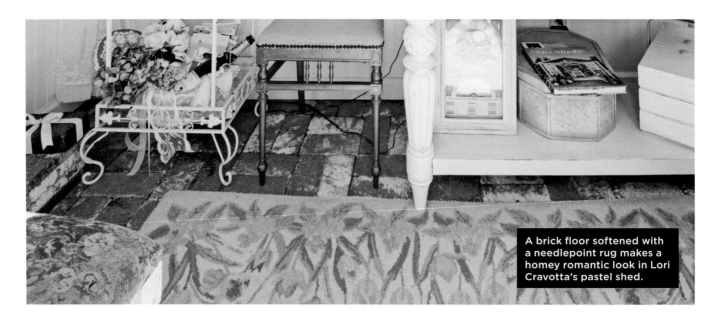

A brick floor softened with a needlepoint rug makes a homey romantic look in Lori Cravotta's pastel shed.

Colored concrete floors take some effort and preparation, but the final results are well worth it. You can custom blend any color you want and add it to the wet concrete before pouring.

Best Shed Flooring Ideas

Here are some shed-friendly flooring options to consider.

- **Rustic/salvaged wood.** Many she sheds have floors made with wood planks salvaged from other uses— barn floor planks, scaffolding, or even wood straight from the tree. The wood is either a lucky find or comes from lumberyards that offer reclaimed lumber in soft and hard species. Pacific Coast Lumber in California, for example, supplies she shed builder A Place to Grow/Recycled Greenhouses with raw lumber from fallen trees. They in turn mill it into floor planks and siding. The product looks antique yet has a consistency in profile that makes it easier to install. Floorboards are milled with and without tongue-and-groove (the latter is a bit more expensive).

- **Laminate and vinyl.** Laminate has come a long way in the last 10 years, offering designs and textures that closely resemble natural materials such as wood, brick, and stone. Laminate can be installed over plywood or concrete, as long as the surface is smooth and dry. You can use self-adhesive laminate squares or large sheets that are cut to fit and set with adhesive. Always carefully follow the manufacturer's instructions. Vinyl has similar options, including floating planks, which you simply "click" into place using interlocking tongues and grooves. Vinyl flooring may wear better in moist conditions than laminate; however, it is more expensive.

- **Cement.** If you're building your shed on a concrete slab, then the slab can do double duty as your floor! Consider staining it for an ultra-modern, loft-in-the-city effect. Meticulous preparation results in even staining without any unsightly scuff marks showing through. Follow the stain manufacturer's instructions very carefully and don't take shortcuts. Concrete paint is another colorful option.

Crystal-clear polycarbonate panels framed with a grid of truss beams produce a shimmering ceiling. A small hanging chandelier provides a feminine touch.

Beautifully stained ceiling planks are reflected in the collection of mirrors placed high on Anita Rackerby's walls.

Ceiling Style

With all this talk about what's beneath our feet, let's not forget to look up! From the fifteenth century onward, ceiling decoration has been an important consideration within the greater houses and castles of the world. In particular, elaborate frescoes and murals depicted religious scenes. Structural elements of a ceiling—namely, the beams and joists—become part of the decorative scheme when they are highlighted with paint or stain.

The ceiling, especially in a shed, is often considered as nothing more than the underside of the very important roof, which keeps the weather outside. And yet there are many ways to give it a dramatic impact without a lot of work. Exposed structural elements such as trusses and crossbeams are very much a part of the shed vernacular. They're also great for displaying textiles and string lights and for hanging interesting artifacts.

Because one of the best things about a she shed is having quiet time to relax, you'll find yourself staring up at the ceiling more than you might think. Make sure this important structural element is part of the planning for something wonderful that you never get tired of gazing at. Use a favorite color in either paint or stain, or various materials such as stamped metal panels, to give your ceiling some added interest.

Not everything has to be miniature in a she shed. Riki Schumacher's china cabinet is quite grand and takes up most of the back wall. Luckily, it pays its own way with deep shelves and cabinet space.

Furnishings

Furniture provides the greatest infusion of personal style within a she shed. It's here that all the dreams and visions for a livable, personal space culminate. You are selecting the pieces you will touch and use—a desk, a chair, a daybed—deciding where they go and how they will look.

At 8' × 10', this shed is on the smaller side, but owner Jennifer Smith made room for a very inviting small sofa for relaxing. It's located on the shadier side of the shed to keep cool in the summer.

Once again, the purpose of your shed dictates, to a large extent, the types of furnishings necessary for utility, pleasure, and comfort. Gardeners need a potting bench, storage area, shelves, and lots of hooks for tools. Quilters need a large tabletop near an electrical outlet for the quilting machine and deep shelves for fabrics. Small business owners need a desk and file drawers. Loafers and dreamers need a comfortable daybed or sofa. What follows are some guidelines and suggestions for the main pieces of furniture you'll be considering.

Seating

Is it just for you, or will the she shed be a gathering space for guests? A small shed may have just enough space for one, but keep in mind the area just outside the shed. In fine weather this could be the right place for a cozy circle of chairs and perhaps a comfortable bench.

If you do have room inside, create an inviting circle or at least two seats facing each other for conversation. Use the available space appropriately; a larger shed can accommodate an upholstered armchair, for example, perhaps with a facing loveseat or small sofa. For smaller sheds, simply place facing seats on opposite sides against the walls. Building window seats is another great option! (This should be decided when drawing up plans for the shed so that bay windows can be included in the design.)

Lounging

We all do our share of lounging! Figuring out the perfect place to read, relax, and nap is hardwired into our brains. The trick is to work out an area that is large enough to stretch out in and to not overspend on a bed or couch that fits. For sheds with an upper loft, well, the work is done. A loft with a sturdy ladder provides a wonderful nest that is very private and cozy, because it is somewhat enclosed. Fit

in a good foam mattress and dress in gorgeous bed coverings with lots of plump pillows. You can even make a small shelf up there for a reading light and water glass.

If no loft can be had, you can make a simple bed platform out of wood that is the right size for the shed. Another idea is a drop-down bench/bed built right into the wall. Even a camping cot will do the trick, as long as you layer it with wonderful linens, pillows, and throw blankets.

Working

For the workspace, the shed should have comfortable seating that faces a table or workbench. Comfort without bulk is the object for your primary seat. With that in mind, a well-made office chair might be the best choice if you plan to spend many hours in it. Dress it up with cute pillows, or do a seat and back recover.

If something less office-y is more to your liking, you should still make sure that comfort and support come first. First, consider a chair you already have. A spare side chair or dining chair can be suitable for work. Consider a slipcover or reupholstering to complement the interior of the shed.

Stools and barstools fit easily into the shed and are comfortable for some, especially artists who need flexibility and move around; they may not be best for computer work, though.

(Above) Carol Cook's art studio/shed is lined floor to ceiling with sturdy shelves. She stores her many art and crafting books there, along with baskets holding smaller items.

(Opposite) Fitting snugly into one side of this tiny she shed, a wrought-iron loveseat is big enough to seat two. Look for great vintage seat frames and splurge on new, comfortable cushions in your favorite fabric.

Dual-Purpose Furnishings

Next time you're shopping for she shed furniture, look for pieces that do double duty. These pieces are well worth getting because they accomplish two things for the space of one. Think stools and ottomans with tops that open up for storage, or a folding table with drawers underneath the top. Other ideas to put on your search list include nesting tables, stacking bins, chalkboard/room dividers, and futon chairs/beds.

My favorite double-duty item for the shed is nesting tables. These wonderful pieces are small-scale and fit underneath each other when not in use. You can find vintage nesting tables at vintage fairs, thrift shops, and antique shops.

A small windowsill is used to store a caddy of flower vases. To hang herbs, simply install a shower or drapery rod across the roof beams and use S hooks.

Storing

Shelving is probably the most popular way we store items in she sheds. Shelves hug the wall and provide good organization while allowing us to see what we have.

Here are some common necessities that sit well on shelves:

- Books
- Gardening supplies
- Dishes and glasses
- Decorative displays
- Clocks and lighting

Another storage method that works well in the shed is cubby clusters. Cubbies are a cross between shelves and bins. They offer horizontal shelving but are deep enough to hold baskets, which are used for unruly items that don't stay put on standard-sized shelves. Think knitting supplies, art supplies, paperwork, and groups of small items.

Storage should be part of nearly any piece of furniture in the she shed. Whether it's cabinets, drawers, shelves, or hooks, be sure to look for storage function, because you're going to need it. And don't forget about some very low-cost ways to incorporate storage using structural elements such as lofts, beams, windowsills, and door backs. Storage done well can be really pretty!

Simple Window Treatment

Most windows go undressed in a she shed. However, if you want a bit of softness framing the glass, try this simple design. Using pretty dishtowels and a long stick found on her property, Kathy Hurwitz made an almost-instant set of curtains for her she shed window.

Materials

- Long stick (look for a stick that's interesting but mostly straight; see Step 1)
- Curtain rod holders or hooks (2 per window)
- Dishtowels (4 per window)

Tools

- Eye and ear protection
- Work gloves
- Tape measure
- Utility knife
- Power drill or screwdriver

1 Kathy measured her window width and found a stick that extended a few inches farther on each side. She stripped off all small shoots and leaves with a utility knife. With a drill and the accompanying hardware, she attached a rod holder on each side of the window, making sure they were the same height, and placed the stick on the rod holders.

2 To make curtains like the ones shown here, twist a dishtowel around the stick, then take the short end and form a loose knot. Tuck the loose end behind the knot.

3 Repeat with the other dishtowels and arrange symmetrically on each side of the window.

Mod Ottoman

The ottoman, a wonderful Turkish gift to the world, is the perfect furnishing for a she shed. It's versatile, because you can prop your feet up on it or use it as a low table. Rebecca Ittner's version shown here has a third use—there's stylish storage inside the vintage suitcase. She made this ingenious little piece using a midcentury modern fabric and a hot glue gun—no sewing necessary.

Materials

- Paint degreaser
- Rags
- Vintage suitcase
- Chalked paint
- Chalked paint sealing wax
- 4 furniture legs, 3" to 4" tall
- Heavyweight art board
- 2 yards fabric
- Batting
- Strong-hold glue sticks

- 3 to 4 yards trim (this will be used around the top interior and padded top of the ottoman)
- 2 pieces plywood, ¾" thick, cut to fit the bottom interior and top surface of the ottoman
- 4 angled mounting plates and screws for furniture legs
- Foam cushion, 1" thick
- Upholstery staples
- Construction glue
- Sandpaper, medium grit

Tools

- Eye and ear protection
- Work gloves
- Scissors
- Paintbrushes
- Ruler or tape measure

- Heavy-duty hot glue gun
- Pencil
- Power drill or screwdriver
- Upholstery staple gun

1 Using paint degreaser or a similar product and rags, Rebecca cleaned the exterior surfaces of the suitcase and let them dry. With scissors, she removed the interior lining of the suitcase, trying to keep the lining intact for measuring new interior components. The interior was cleaned as much as possible.

2 She applied chalked paint to the exterior and any interior sections that would not be covered with fabric. (It took three coats of paint to completely disguise the original blue surface of this suitcase.) Each coat was allowed to dry thoroughly, then lightly sanded to achieve a smooth surface. The paint was then sealed with two coats of chalked paint sealing wax applied according to the manufacturer's directions.

3 Rebecca painted the furniture legs with chalked paint and allowed them to dry, again sealing the dry paint with chalked paint sealing wax.

Interior

4 Rebecca measured the interior of the suitcase top, bottom, and sides and cut art board to these measurements. For the sides of the bottom of the suitcase, she cut two equal-length strips, each half the length of the total length needed, using the old lining pieces as templates.

5 She then measured and cut fabric to cover the cut art board, leaving an extra 1" all the way around each piece in order to adhere them properly.

6

7a

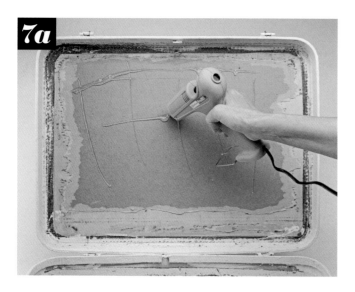

7b

6 Batting was cut to cover the top and bottom pieces; at least ¼" extra was included all around. Rebecca then used a hot glue gun to adhere the batting to the top and bottom pieces. Laying the cut fabric face down on a clean surface, she placed the corresponding padded art board piece in the center and adhered the fabric with hot glue, pulling tightly as she went.

7 The back of the top piece was then adhered to the inside top of the suitcase with hot glue. Rebecca applied the hot glue very generously to ensure a strong bond.

8 Next, she cut the trim to fit around the interior top, plus 2". On each end of the trim, she folded over 1" and used the glue gun to adhere the edges. (This ensured a clean edge once the trim was in place.) The trim was then added using the glue gun.

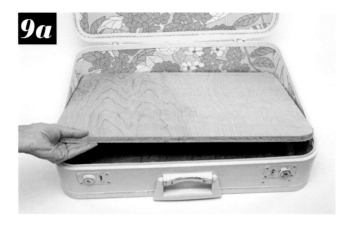

9a

9b

9 Rebecca adhered the strips of fabric-covered art board to the sides of the bottom section. Working quickly, she generously applied hot glue to the bottom interior section, then placed cut plywood on top and pressed down to ensure a tight bond. She generously applied hot glue to the surface of the wood, quickly placing the fabric-covered piece onto the wood and holding it in place until dry.

Exterior

10 To check the placement of the table legs, Rebecca turned the suitcase upside down. After screwing the legs into the mounting plates, she placed them on the bottom of the suitcase and marked the placement of the screw holes with a pencil.

11 She unscrewed the furniture legs from the mounting plates, then used a drill to screw the mounting plates to the bottom of the suitcase where marked.

10

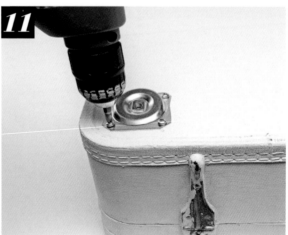

11

Cushion

12 Rebecca cut the foam cushion to fit on the plywood for the top of the ottoman, then adhered the cushion to the plywood with hot glue.

13 She cut batting and fabric to cover the foam cushion, including 2″ extra all around. Then she placed the cut fabric face down on a clean surface, placed the batting on top of the fabric, then placed the cushion face down on the layered batting and fabric. Using the staple gun, she attached the batting and fabric to the bottom of the wood, pulling tight as she went.

14 After applying a generous amount of construction glue to the top of the suitcase, Rebecca set the covered cushion onto the glue, pressed it into place, and allowed it to dry according to manufacturer's directions.

15 She cut trim to fit around the edges of the cushion, plus 2″. She folded each end over by 1″ and used hot glue to fasten down the edges. Then she adhered the trim around the cushion using the glue gun.

Ink Stamp Wall Design

I'm a stencil enthusiast and wanted to do a simple design for the interior walls of my little shed. One day, I came across a fun alternative to stenciling: ink stamp design. I was captivated by the soft, antique-like results. The kit I used has about 12 stamps of various sizes and shapes, including a pretty corner stamp. The most difficult parts for me were figuring out the right amount of ink to load the stamps with and keeping the stamps steady on the wall.

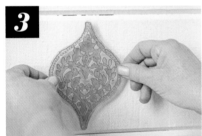

Materials

• Stamps

• Ink sponge

• Stamping ink

• Wet wipes

Tools

• Tape measure

• Pencil

• 8" × 8" ceramic tile or sturdy plastic sheet

1 I selected the stamp designs I wanted to use and removed them from the plastic sheet. Then I planned a design for each section of my wall and marked the center of each section with a pencil. Another way to mark where you want to stamp is to place a couple of dots around the stamp or even outline the entire stamp.

2 Inking the stamp takes a bit of guesswork and testing. You want to distribute the ink evenly so that it's not too wet anywhere. With the smooth side of the stamp design firmly on a tile (or on plastic), I patted the ink sponge on the stamping ink and then on the raised design, getting light and even distribution. I patted for about 20 to 30 seconds and checked carefully that all surfaces were inked.

3 Grasping the stamp on both sides and positioning it carefully, I lined up the bottom point to my pencil mark and then gently laid the stamp against the wall surface.

4 Keeping one hand on the stamp at all times, I pressed gently around the entire surface of the design with my other hand. Occasionally, I lifted the corners of the design to make sure the design was transferring properly.

5 I removed the stamp carefully and let the ink dry. I kept the stamps clean with wet wipes while working and washed them with soap and water if there was excessive ink buildup.

Herringbone Pattern Brick Floor

One of the best things about a brick floor in a she shed is that it does double duty as a foundation. Other good reasons to have a brick floor? It is pretty and easy to maintain, and it feels good underfoot. This version doesn't use mortar. You are going to prepare your she shed site much as you would prepare for a concrete slab, using gravel and sand to "grip" the bricks and surround it with a wood or plastic edging.

Materials

- Paver gravel
- Paver sand
- Plastic or wood edging
- Old or new bricks

Tools

- Eye and ear protection
- Work gloves
- Shovel
- Large level
- Length of 2 × 4 or 4 × 4 (optional)
- Bow rake
- Hammer
- Stakes
- 4" angle grinder with diamond blade
- Broom

1 Prepare the site for brick-laying. It must be as level as possible. In the photos you see here, my husband and I dug out a small tree, some flowerbeds, and lawn to create a 6' × 8' rectangle. Fill in low areas with dirt and continue to dig out high areas until the surface is even. I placed my level in several areas to check as I worked. **Tip:** For better accuracy, place the level on a length of 2 × 4 or 4 × 4.

2 We filled the surface with gravel and smoothed it, using a bow rake, until it was evenly covered.

3 Using paver sand, we poured mounds in several spots within the surface and distributed it with the rake. I continued to work with the level and rake until the surface was level. The sand layer should be about ¼" to ½" thick to grab the bricks.

4 I placed edging around the perimeter of the surface and hammered in stakes to secure it.

5 Starting in one corner, I began laying out a simple herringbone pattern with the bricks. (Refer to the diagram beside photo 5 as a guide.) Some of the bricks had to be cut in half. We used a diamond blade on a 4" grinder to cut them, but you can also figure out how many half bricks you will need and get them cut professionally.

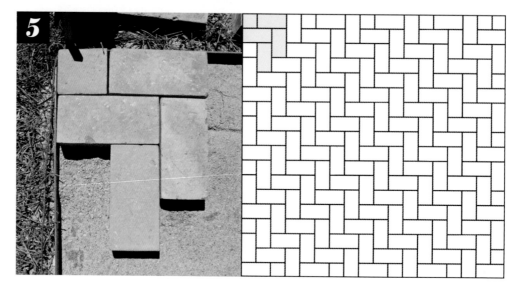

6 I continued working my pattern, keeping the bricks straight and close together, until the surface was covered.

7 For the final step, I poured fine sand over the bricks and swept away excess, repeating this a couple of times until the cracks were well filled.

Part I

Weaving a Wild Vine She Shed

Sheds are usually humble buildings, but most have a floor, walls, ceiling, and roof, right? For this project, we'll stray a bit from convention. In fact, the very essence of a she shed may come not from what is there, but from what isn't. This ultimate organic she shed was created by Ellen Marcus, who used wild kudzu vines for walls and a canvas panel for a ceiling. She put it on a low-rise wood platform, though you can also use a preexisting concrete pad.

Materials

- About 40 grape or kudzu vines
- Scaffolding or frame (such as an old arbor or swing set)
- Natural fiber string

Tools

- Eye and ear protection
- Work gloves
- Protective clothing (long-sleeved denim shirt, denim pants)
- Heavy-duty loppers
- A-frame ladder

Vine-Gathering Tips

- Clearing a thicket of grapevines is much easier with two people; one tugs while the other cuts away resisting vegetation attached to the vine.
- The more unique the base of the vine, the more interesting the structure. Look for mature vines that are gnarled and weathered.
- Vines are nimble and quick to whip back, so expect to be lashed and dress accordingly (avoid wearing knits). To prevent vines from whipping, gently release tension on the vine, and do not bend against the vine's natural curve.

Tip: Ellen wove around the supports, integrating the scaffolding into the finished structure to reinforce it. Another option is to work around the scaffolding so that it can be removed once the structure is completed.

3

1 Ellen and her crew gathered, cut, and pulled living vines from surrounding growth using heavy-duty loppers. They stripped the vines of their leaves, keeping the vines stretched and separate so that they did not tangle. The thickest and longest vines formed the skeleton for the structure.

2 Working with the natural curve of the three most substantial and longest vines, Ellen draped them over the top of the scaffolding and interwove them according to their curves. You'll need a sturdy ladder to do this step. As the thinner ends become more flexible, they can be braided. She used natural fiber string to secure the vines where needed.

3 Next, she made wreaths out of vines and wove them into the vine base. If you do the same, try not to bend against the natural direction of growth, because it weakens the vine. The larger wreaths formed the base support for the structure; plenty of length was left so that it would rest firmly on the ground.

4 Ellen went for the essence of a dome shape, yet the vines are organic, so she knew the shape would be too. She followed the lead of the natural direction of the vines.

5 As the structure nears completion, there's not much more to do besides leaving an opening large enough for an entrance.

Part II

Canvas Cover

A simple waterproof fabric cover is an easy way to turn this natural shed into a more versatile structure. Stitch fabric panels together with a heavy-duty sewing machine, or simply use fabric glue or hook-and-loop fasteners. Don't pass up the opportunity to add a splash of color and interest to the cover—add a single dye color or several. This is your blank canvas!

Materials

- Raw undyed fabric (canvas or cotton duck)
- Nails
- Fabric dye
- Fabric waterproofing spray or organic beeswax
- Hook-and-loop fastener strips

Tools

- Eye and ear protection
- Work gloves
- Hammer
- Clothespins (if using clothesline)
- Paint sprayer
- Garden hose with mister nozzle
- 5-gallon buckets (one for each dye color)
- Extension cord
- Heavy-duty scissors

Canvas Cover Tips

- Tie-dye yours the traditional way by scrunching, fastening with rubber bands, and submerging in large dye buckets instead of spraying.
- For a stronger covering, sew the panels together and create a tent cover.
- Don't want to sew? Purchase an awning tent and drape it over the shed for shade and protection from rain.

1 Ellen started by stretching the fabric between two trees and attaching it at the top with heavy nails. (If you have a clothesline, you could attach the fabric to it with clothespins instead.) With a garden hose, she misted the fabric with water until it was damp but not saturated.

2 The dye was mixed in a bucket (one bucket per color) according to the manufacturer's instructions. Ellen loaded the paint sprayer bucket with dye. (You'll probably need an extension cord to plug in the paint sprayer, depending on where you do this.) With sweeping motions, she sprayed the dye onto the wet fabric, alternating with additional colors.

3 To create a faded tie-dye effect, Ellen gently misted the wet dye with the garden hose. She then let the fabric dry completely and applied waterproofing spray.

4 She cut the panels to the appropriate lengths to drape over the top of the shed and applied hook-and-loop fastener strips to connect the edges.

Cubby Storage

The greatest thing about cubby boxes is that they are very easy to fit into any space. You can fill the whole wall with a group of them, place three side by side under a window, or put one here and one there. If done well, your cubby boxes will look cool even while they're being useful. Here are some basic steps for getting your cubbies in a row.

1 Start by measuring the wall and sketching a design of what you want.

2 Source the cubbies, find antique crates, or build your own boxes to the desired measurements.

3 Mount the cubbies to the walls with screws.

Caroline Borgman and her husband measured the space to figure out how many boxes were needed to create an entire wall of cubbies. Caroline liked them so much she also put some underneath her worktop.

5 | *Doorways & Entryways*

Gone are the days of the drab little shed lurking in the side yard. A she shed is meant to be shown off as the jewel of the landscape. Done well, a she shed draws the eye with interesting construction. It's a supporting actress to gardens and other important backyard features. Everything from size to materials, color, and placement is important to how well the shed complements its surroundings, and vice versa.

The entrance of a she shed is warm and welcoming. It entices and entrances. The door you choose signifies that this is a habitable space. From that door stems the overall framework of the landscaping that surrounds the shed. An entryway, with perhaps a deck or a porch, and a very clear walkway to the shed, provide the eye with clues that this structure is an intentional part of the garden. Your style and landscape arrangement suggest a space where both abundant creativity and serious repose are the orders of the day.

All human beings respond deeply to the lure of a journey. This explains the appeal of trails, pathways, and entrances that intrigue and delight. This rural she shed has it all, beginning with a vine-covered arbor that frames the final destination.

Pay lavish attention to your door and your entryway. Even if your budget isn't so rich, there are lots of simple techniques to create a view that spectators will find irresistible. Your design may not happen overnight, but the following pages offer both easy projects to do right away and ideas for cultivating a richer landscape in the future.

The Doors

The front door comprises ⅓ to ½ the total wall area of most sheds. That means the door should be sturdy and easy to operate. Architect Bob Borson calls the front door "the first exclamation point of the entry procession." And yet sometimes it doesn't get the attention it should.

Think first of what a typical shed door looks like. Toolsheds and storage sheds usually have extra-wide double doors to allow access for large items such as gardening equipment. They're reinforced with cross pieces, and they close with a lock and latch. Windows are rare.

Now, picture the wide door profile of a traditional shed in the more sophisticated form of double French doors. These popular doors, featuring a grid of glass lites (usually two or three across and five down), are welcoming and architecturally interesting. They also let in light through more than half of the door's surface area. For she sheds relying mostly on natural light (as opposed to electric), this is an important consideration.

From there, let your imagination soar, keeping in mind the shed style you hope to create. If it's a simple rustic shed you're going after, then your door might resemble the traditional shed style of two wide doors—but made

French doors are probably the most popular choice for today's she sheds. The design of this urban studio takes the staid French door up a notch with a vibrant yellow finish. Lush ivy and climbing flowers surround it.

from repurposed barn wood instead of cheap plywood. Sheds with a distinct architectural style, such as cottage or Victorian, might be finished with a milled wood door to match.

Finally, don't forget the wonderful details found in good hardware and accessories. Soften a dark wood door with a pair of sparkling crystal doorknobs. Splurge on hammered bronze hinges or adhere a few French appliqués to a plain two-panel door before staining it.

Designing Your Door

Certain styles of doors look best with a matching architectural style. As in other chapters, consider these five she shed styles and note the corresponding suggestions for a perfect front door. You'll need to be practical too, keeping in mind budget, shed size, roof height, swing space, and your desire for privacy.

Jennifer Smith's front door combines two great she shed styles: Dutch and French. Its soft white color complements the shed's serene interior design.

Eclectic. As the word conveys, eclectic is an artful mix of seemingly disparate styles. It provides the greatest freedom in terms of selecting a door style, but it's not always as easy as it sounds. One way to find an eclectic door is to look for it—in secondhand shops, that is. Somehow, when you pair a unique vintage door of any style with an eclectic shed, the marriage just seems to work. As a finish, consider a rich color or perhaps a decorative effect such as faux painting or stenciling.

Garden/Green. The gardening/potting shed is proud of its workhorse heritage and isn't fussy about details. That's precisely the reason it looks so right in the backyard, no matter what. If the shed is used more for potting and a place to stash tools, go practical with a painted wood door that you can install apron and tool hooks on. If you plan to propagate seedlings or grow plants inside, then consider something that lets in sunlight, such as a single French door.

Modern/Zen. As striking as they may be, modern she sheds tend to blend into their surroundings. Unfussy lines and restraint with decorative "things" are the definitive elements that nevertheless have a quiet beauty of their own. Two door styles work well for the modern shed—a door (or double door) with a single large pane of glass, or a track door made with stained wood pieces.

Romantic/Shabby. For this soft, ethereal style, a milled door with fanciful carvings works well. Another great door choice is the Dutch door; the top section might have French or diamond-paned windows in it. Paint with a distressed patina (do this by layering two different paint colors, then lightly sanding through the top coat here and there).

Rustic. Keep things simple for your rustic shed. A fancy door just doesn't convey the right message of "I'm happiest with the bare essentials." Simple can actually be the most beautiful choice available. If you are restoring an old shed, perhaps you can make over the original door so that it is a cheerful, cleaned-up version of its former self. If the shed is new or the door is beyond saving, then a track door or a Dutch door designed in the barnyard style will look right at home.

An off-center sliding glass door is discreet and blends well with the dark gray of Alexis King's home office.

Entryways and Landscaping

The area surrounding a shed's front door should be as carefully considered as the structure itself. When gazing at a she shed, the eye takes in the front facade with its windows and doorway as well as the immediate framework created by the landscape. Fencing, trees, shrubbery, garden areas, lawn, swimming pool, back porch, decking—all may play a part in adding to (or detracting from) the she shed's site location.

In a perfect world, the she shed is built on a small rise of land, far enough from the main house for privacy, surrounded by mature trees and gardens. No bland stucco walls or utility lines are in sight, just pastoral views as far as the eye can see. Unfortunately, this situation is extremely rare. Most she shed owners will need to be creative and resourceful to create a visually appealing spot. They will also need to work around the elements they already have.

Site Selection

There are both practical and aesthetic considerations for siting your she shed. Here are some important ones.

- Many cities and neighborhoods have rules about how far a structure needs to be from the property line, how many square feet it is, and how high the roof can be. Research your area's rules before investing time planning a site.

- Consider your rainfall and the drainage of your property. Keep the she shed away from (or above) areas that get a lot of accumulated moisture.

- What are your foundation options? Perhaps you have a concrete surface already in the backyard. Could it support a she shed?

The journey to artist Carol Cook's little gem of a she shed is as fun as arriving at the destination. Elevate the humblest of sheds by surrounding it with intriguing pathways, visually appealing clusters of foliage, and, here and there, a place to sit and rest.

- Plan the relationship to the main house. The she shed strikes a nice pose when it faces the back of the house, but that isn't the only way to go. Think about proximity too; you want the she shed close enough for convenient walking back and forth, but not so close that it crowds the physical space around the home.

Once these basics have been covered, a plan that may include hardscape and plantings can be hatched. Strive to integrate the landscape design you already have and, if necessary, seek the advice of a professional garden designer. Sometimes having a fresh pair of eyes will illuminate ideas you haven't yet considered.

The perfect situation for any shed is on a slight rise in the yard. Kim and Justin Brandstater took advantage of a concrete platform that already existed from their children's old playhouse to build this she shed. Decorative fencing and a wooden gate add a sense of permanence.

The 5 Best Places for a She Shed

The she shed owner usually does not have the luxury of choosing from myriad perfect locations in her backyard. She must work toward the best, perhaps even the only, practical solution. Here are five areas or conditions that could help narrow it down.

1. She sheds work well in the final frontier (i.e., the very back) of the backyard. The shed adds definition to the property line and enjoys plentiful landscaped area in front of it. Lots of attention will be needed for pathways, and you'll want some color or other decorative elements on the shed to make it pop.

2. A well-centered she shed lends symmetry to the backyard, allowing for gardens to surround it in a very picturesque way. If the house is not quite centered, you may want to place the shed at a diagonal so that the front facade is visible from the house.

3. There's nothing at all wrong with a solid, dependable concrete slab or a brick pad for the she shed. However, sheds on raised foundations provide a "skyline" that can greatly enhance the yard's overall landscape.

4. Do you have a preexisting foundation? It's somewhat contrary to #3, but it's something to pay attention to if you have one. You'll need a very good reason to ignore a site that is already level, has good drainage, and is ready for building.

5. They say good fences make good neighbors; sometimes she sheds do too. Consider placing your she shed in a spot that doesn't have fences or shrubbery for adequate privacy screening. Be sure and clear it with affected neighbors before building; chances are they'll be just as glad to have their privacy improved too!

Extensive brick paving connects this large she shed to the main house. Everything about this entrance—double French doors, clean color palette, meticulous masonry—conveys the security of a well-cared-for backyard sanctuary.

This picturesque landing in Jennifer Smith's backyard has the advantage of splendid mature oak trees surrounding it. Jennifer's impressive talent as an interior decorator is evident in how well she positioned the shed to feel both accessible and tucked away. Although situated flat on the ground, the shed appears anchored and looks as if it's always been there.

Decks, Porches, and Stoops

Just like a house, a shed can benefit very much from a "landing" that acts as a transition from the outside to the inside. The three most common forms are decks, porches, and stoops. Decks are open wood platforms built in front of or around a structure, used for walkways and for outdoor living. Porches are often covered platforms with posts and railings, also intended to extend the living space of a house or shed. Stoops are small landings with steps to allow easy entrance and exit from a building. These areas finish off the shed beautifully, lending a sense of permanence and sophistication. A she shed is best suited for a deck built on a raised foundation, hillside, or slope and has sufficient clearance from other structures or hardscapes.

Linda Carvahlo built an expansive deck floating above the level yard surface. The overhang extends as far as the deck does, providing good shelter from rainy weather.

Stylish Ideas for the Ground-Level She Shed

If your shed is planted firmly on flat ground, don't worry. (Mine is too!) The important thing is to make the shed feel established and intentional, not plopped down. There are lots of fun ways to do this.

Define the area. If possible, create a shaped area (circular, square, or freeform) about 3 to 4 feet wider than the she shed. Softscape can be a green lawn or mulch with interesting plantings; think succulents and tropicals with a modern-style shed or flowering shrubs for traditional-, cottage-, or romantic-style sheds.

Vertical gardens. Treat the shed as a garden sculpture—think obelisk or statuary. Train vines against it, install window boxes and bracketed shelves for potted plants, and establish dwarf trees and flowers as close to the perimeter as possible.

Layer. An effective way to get dimension is to layer plants by height. Begin with taller shrubs and flowers directly against the walls of the shed, then graduate to

(Left) Rebecca Lynne Spencer created a simple oval area around her blue shed and filled it in with bark mulch. This low-budget solution was enough to set off the recently restored shed so that it became a focal point on the property.

(Right) Liz Ridgway's rustic potting shed is brightened by small containers of plants and flowers just outside the entrance.

smaller plants working outward. It makes the shed appear like it "grew" out of the ground too.

Container gardens. The easiest trick in the book is container gardening—and it looks terrific just about everywhere around a shed. Bank pretty pots around the doorway and line them up across from each other to create a pathway. Hang them from rafter beams and park them on small tables.

"Float" a deck. A ground-level deck is still possible, if your shed's door threshold is at least 6 inches above the ground. A floating deck hovers just slightly over concrete or sod, with just enough room for airflow. Ask your contractor about options that are appropriate for your area's weather conditions.

Even in this narrow backyard, a side deck fit cleverly onto Jirapa Cocking's ultra-modern she shed. She and her husband, Steven, used decking wood topped with anti-slip stain in American Mahogany.

Track Door

Jeff and Lynn Robson completely renovated an old shed on their Michigan property. The original facade had no door and two small windows. They reframed the side, removed the windows, and put in a new header for a large doorframe. Purchased track and roller hardware combined with salvaged barn wood resulted in this handsome and substantial shed door. The two doors open to a maximum of 92 inches.

Materials

- 2 × 6" treated tongue-and-groove boards
- Nails
- Track and roller kit
- Clamping interior door latch
- Door handles
- Flexible weather strips

Tools

- Eye and ear protection
- Work gloves
- Hammer
- Tape measure
- Pencil
- Power drill
- Level

1 The Robsons constructed their door using tongue-and-groove car siding wood boards salvaged from their family hog farm, which was recently torn down. The tongue-and-groove worked nicely to bind and hold the material tightly together to minimize warping and allow for minimal bracing, keeping the door square and flat. They made each door just over half the size of the door opening, which is 8'. They placed crossbraces on the upper and lower sections of each door and screwed them in place.

2 Jeff located the center of the opening in the shed to start the measuring process for the track placement.

3 They laid out the track with the rollers temporarily placed on the door using a flat surface. This helped verify the placement of all the components to provide the full desired door movement and opening. It also prevented measurement errors.

4 Following the instructions from the manufacturer, Jeff installed the end stops on the track and placed the track in position under the door rollers at the stop to measure the distance from the edge of the door to the mounting hole in the track. This gave him the distance the track needed to be placed back away from the center of the opening.

5 He then positioned the door in the opening at the desired height to get the measurement of the track placement when the door was installed in the opening. This determined how far above the opening the track should be installed.

6 Jeff marked the location for the end mounting hole of the track away from the door opening center. He then marked the distance above the opening on this previous line to locate the hole for the first mounting screw. He installed the lag screw to place the track above the opening.

7 Placing a level on the track above the door, he marked the additional mounting holes to install the lag screws for the track.

8 Jeff installed the additional track mounting screws and placed the door on the track to check for proper sliding and to verify that the door stopped at the center of the opening. He adjusted the track stop bumpers somewhat to allow for full movement of the door.

9 He repeated the steps to install and attach the track for the opposite door at the same height, repeating the process of measuring for the end mounting hole positions and levelness of the track.

10 They tested the door-track installation to make sure it was correct and level, that the doors met evenly at the top, and that the center closing gap was even from top to bottom.

11 They installed a barn door-style clamping interior latch on each door so that the clamping force holds the doors closed at the center. The track end stop bumpers were adjusted to get both doors to stop at the center.

12 They installed handles and locking hardware on the interior for opening. (Try a local farm store for common latches and handles used for outdoor pole building–style sliding doors. The internet will also give a host of hardware choices.) The final touch was putting flexible rubber weather strips (similar to overhead garage doors) around the door opening to close the gaps.

Money-Saving Tip

The Robsons bought a door track designed for a 6' opening rather than 8'. It was less expensive and also kept the track short enough to fit within the width of the shed. Adjustments were made in the placement of the rollers on the door (installed closer together) and the track (placed back from the center of the opening) to allow approximately 46 inches of space per door when the doors were opened fully.

Dutch Door

When building my petite she shed, I struggled to find a door that was narrow enough to fit between the two front windows. Finally, I scored a beautiful old door made of solid wood, and my husband and I set to work transforming it into a Dutch door. I think this is a pretty easy project, but you will need a table saw to cut the door in half.

Materials

- Wood door
- Wood scrap, about 1" × 6"
- Screws
- Sandpaper, 100 to 150 grit
- Primer
- Paint or stain
- 4 door hinges
- 2 doorknobs and door plates
- Wood glue
- Trim, ¾" half-round
- Finish nails

Tools

- Eye and ear protection
- Work gloves
- Power drill
- Tape measure
- Pencil
- Table saw
- Jigsaw
- Router
- Clamps
- Sander
- Paintbrushes or rollers
- Nail gun or hammer

1 The first thing I needed was a door that fit the petite stature of my shed. After sourcing one, we hauled it home, cleaned it up, and removed all the hardware with a drill.

2 I measured the framed opening of the shed, then marked on the door where it would be cut in half. I removed an extra inch to fit the ledge that we would be installing on the bottom half as well.

3 Using the table saw, we cut the door. Cut pieces of wood were placed around the cutline as a guide for the saw. We also had to use the same saw to shave a bit off the top and bottom edges of the door to fit.

4 Next, I made the door ledge with the scrap wood. Its length covered the top of the lower door section, and it was about 6" wide. I made a curve on each end, cutting it out with the jigsaw.

5 Using the router and holding the wood in place with clamps, I carved a small indentation around the edge for decoration.

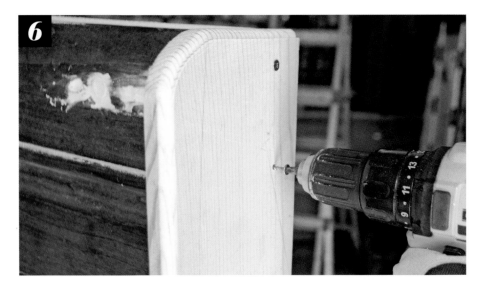

6 I attached the ledge to the door half with wood glue followed by screws.

7 The door was then sanded, using an orbital sander and 150-grit sandpaper (I hand sanded all the door's molding and carving areas). At this time, I primed and painted the bottom and upper edges of the door and let them dry.

8 We installed the door into the frame, making sure to check for fit. Then we secured it in place with hinges and hinge plates.

9 I painted the remainder of the door and let it dry. Then we installed the doorknobs and door plates.

10 We added trim around all sides of the door, attaching it with finish nails and a nail gun. Because of the tight space, our upper and lower trim were added to the door itself.

Vertical Ladder Garden

Because she sheds are often tucked into tight spaces, creative gardening is in order. Deborah Hayes made this vertical planter using an old single-sided ladder and planter pockets made with oilcloth. To enhance drainage, she decided to sew the pockets onto the backing so the seam would leak a bit. Lean it against any wall or on the front porch for a bright spot of color.

Materials

- Vintage single-sided ladder
- Fabric (burlap or oilcloth)
- Thread
- Hook-and-loop fastener tape
- Gravel
- Potting soil
- Plants
- Moss (optional)

Tools

- Tape measure
- Scissors
- Sewing machine
- Trowel

1 Deborah measured the width of the ladder rungs as well as the space between each rung. She added 5" to the length for wrapping around the rung—3" to go around the rung, which was 1¼" in diameter; 1" for hook-and-loop tape width; and 1" for wiggle room.

2 Deborah measured her desired pocket height, then cut fabric double that measurement. This way the printed pattern can be seen from every angle, both inside and outside the pocket.

3 Deborah then folded the pocket back piece lengthwise and stitched all edges together to secure. She repeated this with fabric for the pocket front piece. She measured and attached the hook-and-loop fastener strips at the correct distance at the top of the back pocket fabric so that the fabric wraps and holds securely around the ladder rung.

4a

4b

4 Once all the pockets were finished, Deborah attached them to each rung. She scattered a small amount of gravel into the bottom of each pocket, then a small layer of potting soil. The plants were then inserted and filled in with soil. She finished with some damp moss to keep the soil moist.

4c

Mosaic Stepping-Stone

Stepping-stones are enchanting garden elements that don't require a lot of money or work to install. Kim Brandstater has boxes full of colorful cracked china, glass, and tile fragments that she uses to create intricate mosaic designs using a mold and quick-drying concrete. Create your own designs and make a personalized pathway to your she shed with this ancient art form.

Materials

- Mosaic mold (size and shape of your choosing)
- Butcher or packing paper and pen
- Plates, tiles, stained glass, and glass stones
- Clear contact paper
- Petroleum jelly or cooking spray
- Wire mesh
- Quikrete (or similar quick-drying concrete)

Tools

- Eye and ear protection
- Plastic rubber gloves
- Tile cutters
- Scissors
- Wire cutters
- Bucket for cement
- Trowel
- Sturdy board scrap
- Tile grout sponge
- Small bucket for water
- Towel
- Drop cloth and apron

1 Kim started by placing the mold on a piece of paper and drawing an outline around it; this is where her design would be worked.

2 She used tile cutters to cut plates and tiles until she had enough material for the design. (You can also buy precut tiles and plate mosaics on Etsy and eBay.)

3 Kim built her mosaic design about ¼" inside the outlined area.

Tip: Glass stones should have the flatter side facing up—you'll want as much surface area as you can get in your final design.

4 When the design was finished, Kim cut a piece of clear contact paper 2" larger than the design on all sides. With the help of a friend, she removed the paper backing. She then placed the contact paper over the design and gently pressed all the mosaic pieces onto the paper. She cut the contact paper as close to the design as possible.

5 Kim lubricated the mold on the bottom and sides with petroleum jelly; you can also use cooking spray. Gently lifting the mosaic design (stuck to the contact paper), Kim flipped it over and placed it in the mold upside down. Any fallen pieces were tucked back in at this point. Note that this is the time to do any final adjustments to the design spacing. Once the concrete is poured, that's it!

6 To prepare for the following steps, Kim donned her bib apron and laid a dropcloth outside on a flat surface. With her wire cutters, Kim cut a piece of wire mesh to fit the mold. In the concrete bucket, she mixed Quikrete with water—about 6 cups of concrete mix for a 12" round stone. She poured some mix into the mold to fill it halfway, then placed the wire mesh in. She continued to pour in more concrete until it reached just under the top of the mold, leveling it off with a trowel.

7 With the filled mold on a flat surface, she moved and tapped it on the surface gently for about 5 to 10 minutes to remove any air bubbles. She let it dry for at least 30 minutes. (Drying times will differ depending on the weather; if it is cold outside it might take an hour.)

8 Once the concrete was dry, she put a sturdy board on top of the mold and flipped it over quickly. Then she set it on the dropcloth and removed the mold. She carefully peeled off the contact paper.

9 Dipping a sponge in the bucket of water several times, Kim gently rubbed the surface to clean off the cement that was covering up some of the design. She scraped away the concrete, using a bit more force with the grout sponge, until the full design showed and all the small holes were filled in. She let it dry and then buffed it with a dry towel. Note that the stone needs a few days to completely cure.

Learn the Art of Espalier

Espalier is the horticultural practice of training fruit-bearing trees or vines to grow flat—think of grapevines in a vineyard. The branches are carefully pruned and then tied to wires set in a desired pattern. Within a few years you have an attractive, lacy wall of green that looks great against the she shed, yet requires very little room. Landscape designer Christine Darnell trained an apple tree against her red shed; she says that espalier is just like training any other kind of plant. It takes patience, but you will love the results. Choose the sunniest side of your she shed and get growing!

1 Choose your plant carefully. Check with a trusted local nursery to see what is recommended for your area. Some nurseries will have "starter" espaliered fruit trees so you can get a head start, but they will be relatively expensive compared to a one-gallon tree with few branches.

2 Fruit trees love the sun—they do best with five to six hours of sun per day. Choose a south- or east-facing wall to get the optimum exposure. Plant your tree about 6" from the wall. Your objective is to raise a tree and snip the leader (main stem) at intervals. It will produce buds on either side below the snip, and another main shoot upward. As new growth occurs, select the best shoot and side buds, and snip the rest. The side buds will grow out as branches.

3 Erect your framework of wood, wire, or metal to support the espalier and make sure your leaders are absolutely straight with the desired angles. Christine suggests tying the leader to a bamboo cane as it grows, then securing both cane and leader to the framework. When the branches have reached about 12" in length, train them horizontally by tying them to the framework with something flexible such as twine. The new shoot and buds will grow, and you'll simply repeat the process until you have a ladder of shoots and branches.

4 Keep adjusting the ties, and prune annually during late winter or early spring. Prune fearlessly, especially in the beginning. Use clean, sharp shears to make clean, diagonal cuts on the tree stems. For advanced designs other than horizontal branches, follow the same principles using wire laid out in your desired pattern. **Tip:** Use a trellis in the back of the plant for easy tying and for keeping track of your branch patterns.

6 | *Important Details*

They might be small compared to roofing, walls, and windows, but there is nothing trivial in the impact of great details. The finishing touches you put on your shed are very often infused with more color, creativity, and originality than any other part of the masterpiece. Why? Because artistic details are the things that set human beings apart from all other living species. Many, many creatures make their own shelters, beds, and hiding places; only humans have the yearning for beauty and meaning that go beyond function in their surroundings.

No doubt some of these final touches will call on things you've been carting around for many years. That one brass lamp with the silk shade your grandmother gave to you. A couple of ceramic elephant pots waiting patiently for some sweet peas to be planted in them. The challenge will be in curating; overcrowding is not the objective here.

Small they might be, but stylish details are what turn an ordinary shed into something truly special. They are the frosting on the cake, the special touches that people remember long after they've left the room.

The rest of the decorating will be with items custom made or purchased especially for this new space of yours. Take your time on this part—it will be an incredibly enjoyable phase in shed building that you won't want to rush. Give your eyes time to adjust to the physical layout and the way the sun moves through the shed. Getting to know the nooks and crannies will make the space more familiar and the things you will want to do start falling into place.

Are You Crafty or a Visionary?

The crafty she shed owner wants to do everything herself and avoids ready-made details as much as possible. The visionary isn't so particular about where something comes from; she just wants to have everything look exactly as it does in her mind. Many women are a bit of both. What matters is the joy of stretching your creative muscle a little bit, and that you're building something new for yourself rather than simply an extension of your house.

Sometimes the desire to do it yourself is hampered by fear—it's scary to make things on your own! What if it doesn't turn out right? How do I figure it out?

Start Somewhere

Usually, the best place to start fine-tuning your shed is with your wallet. Buzzkill though it may be, a tight budget is going to dictate what can be done in the near future and what must wait. In a way, it's liberating—a limited budget means you focus on only one or two things at a time.

(Left) You'll look at tools and materials in a whole new way while designing your she shed. Even if you don't have the time or skills to make everything, the artistic muscle inside you will be made stronger during this journey.

The biggest expenditure might be a high-quality area rug. If your flooring is serviceable but not exactly the stuff of dreams, you can transform it with a soft, plush covering that brings out the wall color. On the other hand, the splurge might be for an incredible fabric and professional upholstering to spruce up your favorite chair. Choose your big spend, but choose it wisely.

From there, you have a few options for proceeding with the final details in your shed with an emphasis on meaningfulness and budget friendliness. It might be helpful to look at these details in broad categories so you can start planning.

What to Buy and What to Make

Making something instead of buying it doesn't always save you a lot of money. What it does is provide a greater sense of creative control. Using your hands to make something includes taking raw materials and turning them into a product that wasn't there before. More commonly, though, we get into the upcycling realm, where old castoffs find new life. Perhaps you can make something even better than it was before.

Few people are skilled enough to make furniture, but many can manage a wonderful facelift by repainting a comfortable chair. Restoring and making over items is incredibly satisfying and within the skill set of those with the determination to try. Yes, there is a substantial chance for failure and mistakes. But the benefits, even in the trying, far outweigh the risks.

Artwork

If you are fortunate enough to be an artist yourself, then half of the decorative element of your shed is already settled. Use your shed as a gallery for your showpiece work, whether it is fine art, mixed media, photography, quilting, pottery, or jewelry. The art in your shed should reflect your

(Right) Romantic floral art is one of Vicki Sakioka's favorite finds when she visits vintage fairs and arts communities. Some of her pieces are hung on the wall, like this one (bottom) above a nightstand. Others are on shelves (top), propped casually against the wall.

passion for life, whether it's the work of an imaginative son or daughter or the results of your secret love for potato stamping! Start working on graffiti art, or samples of tattoo art, upon the walls of your shed. It's your canvas.

For the non-artist who nevertheless loves to surround herself with the works of others, there are many ways to go. Usually a more informal approach to artwork works best in a shed, rather than ornate oils in heavy frames. Here are a few ideas to consider:

- For the eclectic shed: Art glass, colorful textiles, and exotic objects from around the world

- For the modern shed: One single, oversized wall covering, and an abstract metal sculpture

- For the gardening shed: Old tools, enamel buckets, and vintage fruit crate labels

- For the romantic shed: Fanciful framed mirrors, small floral paintings, and collectible small antiques

- For the rustic shed: Wonderful carved wood, antique tools, and perhaps a dramatic large mural

Decorative Accessories

Let the fun begin! Decorative accessories are all those special extra elements that catch your eye at decorator showhouses and gift shops. Nearly anything can be a decorative accessory, so the categories here are not all-inclusive. Think of them as items you can certainly live without, but would prefer not to.

Area rugs and cozy throws. The she shed can often be a little rugged, not quite as warm and cozy as the main house. A rug underfoot will help immensely, adding color and cushioning for your feet. Make sure any rugs for the shed are durable and can be washed easily. Continue the cozy with at least one fabulous throw—not your son's beige and orange elementary school fundraiser throw. If you have an old blanket you like, cut it down to throw size, then add a decorative edging. Crochet a scalloped edge or stitch a smooth edge using satin blanket binding.

(Above) Surrounded by a very rustic and restrained aesthetic, this fanciful little chandelier somehow feels just right. Play with contrasts, and don't always play it safe with your stylistic decisions.

(Opposite) Soft and inviting, Jennifer Smith's shed is layered with quiet creams, accented by both painted and natural wood. Her large plush rug helps create a "living room" effect.

Art objects. Not quite hanging art yet equally artful, decorative displays should include lots of different shapes, colors, and textures. Finally, a place to proudly display some of your collections that have been stored for decades!

Fresh flower displays. Small, loosely arranged bouquets placed in a variety of vessels (not necessarily traditional vases) add life and color to any corner. Ideally, your garden provides flowers for you to use, but there are other creative ways to get fresh blooms and greens. Don't

(Left) String lights and rope light illuminate Amy Smith's shed both day and night. She also added a rustic central light fixture made from galvanized metal.

(Right) Substantial casement stay hardware shines attention on Rachel Roe's beautifully framed windows.

(Opposite) Pieces like this old fireplace surround add a lot of character to the simple walls of a she shed without taking up a lot of space. Your shed will no doubt hold a couple of very meaningful pieces from your home or your childhood. Make these pieces a priority when putting your space plan together.

overlook fresh cuttings from the weekly hedge trimming, snipping rosemary or ivy from other parts of the yard, or transferring a few choice flowers from a large arrangement inside the house. Fill in with wild herbs, such as fresh mint, from the grocery store. (Snip a leaf or two for your iced tea.)

Hardware. Whether it's helping to open a window or displayed as an art object, good hardware can be spectacular and always catches an appreciative eye. Hardware includes commonplace items like hinges, brackets, and window latches, as well as all the components for a door (knobs, locksets, and hinges). You will not regret investing in higher quality hardware that not only looks good but functions perfectly too.

Lighting. Accent lighting is a great addition to the she shed if you have the proper wiring. Many women opt to fully wire their sheds if they're to be used for crafting or working. If you do have the wiring installed for lighting, make the most of it. Consider track lighting in the eclectic, gardening, or modern shed, as it can light both the main workspace and dim corners. For the rustic and romantic sheds, a sparkling statement chandelier is the way to go. Rustic sheds can also look wonderful with cowboy-style lanterns, both hanging and on the tabletop. String lights can add a bit of illumination and a lot of style and are quite happy on an extension cord.

Signage. Somewhere along the line, she sheds have become famous for signage. Even if you're not opening up a wine bar or a pop-up shop in the shed, a personalized sign tells the world at large who you are—your humor, beliefs, and sentiments. Hang a sign directly above the door or prop it on a windowsill. If you're a graphic artist or an accomplished hand letterer, then use those skills to draw or paint an original sign that pronounces the name of your shed. Other signage ideas include famous quotes, inspirational phrases, and fun wordplay ("My Shed-teau"). Rugged natural wood makes a great sign base, but consider acrylic or metal as well.

Look at your possessions with new eyes and create pretty stylistic touches such as this dainty arrangement in a teapot.

How to Be a Stylist

Want your she shed to be photo worthy? You never know when the local newspaper or even a favorite garden magazine editor might come to call. Styling is a unique art, and there are a few simple tricks that can really help you set off your decor to its best advantage.

Start by designing for change. We all change tastes and interests, so embrace that by freshening your shed every so often. Keep favorite items together in a closet, and draw from that. Hand in hand with this concept: edit what's on display. Simplicity is essential in a shed where every inch counts. Also, what seems satisfying to the eye will look overcrowded in the lens of a camera. Try editing out a few pieces, and you'll find it turns down the visual volume, adding joy and peace to the scene. You have a lot of favorite things—learn to highlight just a few of them.

Even with minimal items, you can make pretty vignettes by clever grouping. Use your shed's architectural nooks and crannies for placing small gatherings of like items at varying heights. Understand how color, theme, and similar function (clocks, candles, etc.) will pull things together. And don't forget the flowers! Even if you ignore all the other tips, use this one: fresh flower arrangements cure a variety of ills, from mismatched furniture to boring office shelves. Tuck small colorful flower arrangements anywhere it feels right.

Last but not least, celebrate the season by reflecting the colors, florals, and themes of the moment in your shed. Enjoy the opportunity to freshen the interior every couple of months; use leftover decorations from your home, and consider making some of your own. A basket that remains in the shed all year long can get a new dress each season—acorns in the fall, ornaments in the winter, eggs in the spring, seashells in the summer. The shed's scale offers an opportunity to showcase the tiny gems that you love.

Hanging Gardens

Vertical gardens are wonderful around the exterior of a she shed; they also enhance the interior. Feng shui calls for surrounding oneself with green, living things, and here are a few ways to do it in a small space.

(Clockwise from above left) A double hanging basket dresses up the corner of Jennifer Smith's she shed without obstructing any of the views.

Carolyn Dunster, an author and expert in small-space gardening, festoons her London she shed with hanging planters made from leather and canvas. She also makes the most of her small shed's beams for hanging dried herbs.

Rachel Roe places indoor plants high on a bookshelf; the trailing vines creep down attractively along the wood.

If you want to hang herbs, trim them to the desired length, stacking from the longest stem in back to the shortest in front. Then secure bunches by wrapping the twine around the stems, knotting and creating a loop for hanging.

Materials

- Assorted door hardware
- Wood base
- Sandpaper, 100 and 150 grit
- Stain
- Screws
- Picture-hanging wire and hook or nail
- Fresh herbs or flowers, about 6″ long
- Twine

Tools

- Eye and ear protection
- Work gloves
- Sander
- Paintbrush
- Power drill or screwdriver
- Pliers

Door Hardware Herb Display

As pretty as they are useful, door hardware pieces can live a second life beyond the obvious one. Antique door hardware in particular is a real find, as it often exhibits remarkable craftsmanship and pieces are frequently made of fine metal such as brass. If you like to scout around for interesting antiques, start collecting doorknobs, back plates, drawer pulls, and cabinet knobs for this simple wood display. Deborah Hayes demonstrates it for hanging dried flowers or herbs; it would also make a pretty hanging rack for purses and aprons.

1 Assemble various vintage door hardware with knobs, or add knobs. Deborah used vintage back plates with a selection of vintage glass doorknobs.

2 Deborah used a door from a vintage cabinet, but you can use whatever piece of wood you like for mounting. She sanded her wood, starting with the coarser grit (100) and finishing with 150. Then she stained it with a natural colored oil-based stain.

3 Using screws, she mounted the door hardware to the wood. You can use pliers if needed to tighten the knobs on the screws.

4 She installed picture-hanging wire on the back of the wood piece before hanging it and adding the herbs bundled with twine.

More String Light Ideas

- **Tuna cans.** Use clean aluminum tuna cans instead of food molds.
- **Screen cubes.** Fashion little lantern cubes using screen material framed with wood.
- **Plastic "lamp" shades.** Take clear plastic cups and cover with fabric that is decoupaged to the outside of the cup using diluted craft glue. Cut an X on the bottom of the cup and insert string light.
- **Origami.** Use sturdy card stock to make pretty folded cubes around the lights. Keep plenty of room between light and paper.

Materials

- Vintage or new miniature food molds
- String of miniature lights (white or multi)
- Metal glue

Tools

- Eye and ear protection
- Work gloves
- Power drill
- Pilot bit and ¼″ bit
- Metal file

Personalized String Lights

There are thousands of string light ideas online that I find fascinating, but I wanted to try something new. While browsing a large flea market during the summer, I spotted a bin filled with vintage gelatin molds. These gave me an idea: create string light backdrops by drilling a hole in the top of each mold and inserting the light through.

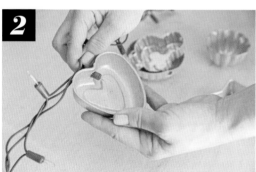

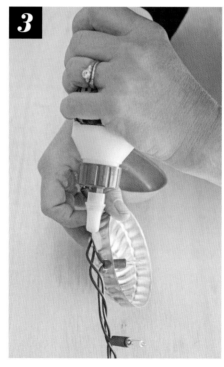

1 I started the hole at the top of each food mold with a pilot bit. Then I used a ¼" bit to make a hole large enough for the light shaft to go through. (When doing this, file any rough edges with a metal file if needed.)

2 I fit the food molds onto every other light, pulling gently until the entire light and shaft came through the hole.

3 Holding the wires on top of the mold, I then placed a couple of drops of metal glue underneath the wires on each side of the hole. Let your glue cure according to the manufacturer's instructions before moving on and attaching the string to the ceiling beams, or where desired.

Materials

- Scrap material
- Masking tape (optional)
- Twill or herringbone tape, 1″ wide
- Thread
- Small nails or pushpins

Tools

- Paper
- Pencil
- Scissors for paper
- Pinking shears or pinking rotary cutter
- Self-healing cutting mat
- Ruler
- Iron
- Pins
- Sewing machine or needle

Cutting Tips

Liz finds using a rotary cutter much easier than traditional scissors. When using a cutter, work with a ruler, cutting along its edge. This will result in a nice, sharp finish for the triangles.

Working in a standup position at a workbench helps with the cutting. You can apply a great deal of downward pressure onto the cutter and get through the material the first time.

Cheery British Bunting

While bunting is popular in many cultures, the English seem to have a particular fondness for this simple trimming. Liz Ridgway, whose company Denys & Fielding creates deck chairs and other home wares using wonderful bright fabrics, surrounds her rustic gardening shed with the classic flag-shaped bunting. She notes that it's a perfect way to reuse old clothing or bedding with sentimental meaning. Liz used a sewing machine, but you can also hand-stitch the bunting to the tape.

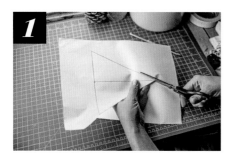

1 Before cutting, Liz made a paper template for the triangular bunting shape and size and cut it out with scissors.

2 Once she created her template, Liz placed it on top of the material and cut it out. You can either draw around the template and then cut with your shears, or, if using a cutter, simply secure the template with a little masking tape on one side. Then, on a cutting mat, using your cutter and a ruler, cut around the template. Remove any excess masking tape once cut.

3 She folded the twill tape in half, making it ½″ wide, then pressed with an iron. Liz placed her bunting pieces into the folded tape at intervals, making sure the shortest side of each triangle was caught within the fold. She secured them with pins as she went.

4 She then sewed the triangles into place, which you can do either using a sewing machine or by hand. If you use a sewing machine, it might be easier to tack the triangles in place rather than using pins.

5 Hang the bunting in place with small nails or pushpins.

Materials

- 5 mm electroluminescent (EL) wire, 10′ or 20′, with battery pack
- Acrylic sheet or white-painted plywood, about 18″ × 18″
- Pencil
- Gel super glue
- White electrical tape
- Small metal chain, about 12″
- 4 S hooks
- 2 screw eyes

Tools

- Eye and ear protection
- Work gloves
- Dry erase marker or pencil
- Power drill
- Drill bits, pilot and ¼″
- Jigsaw

Neon Sign

I have a ridiculous fondness for neon signs, and there is nothing more appealing to me than to drive down the main street of an American town and gaze at the glowing theater marquees and arrow-shaped motel signs. I started looking for a way to incorporate that wonderful glow into a sign for my own shed. Real neon signage requires glass tubes, capturing gas, and high electrical currents. Instead, I went a simpler route with an acrylic sheet and glow wire.

1 Figure out what you want your sign to say, so that you know how much EL wire to get. I purchased 20' and had a lot of wire left over after spelling "EK's Shed." I used some excess to make a frame and a heart. You cannot cut it (at least, not easily), so any unused wire will need to be secured to the sign's back.

2 My desired sign size was 16" × 9", so I marked the shape on the acrylic sheet with a pencil and cut it using a jigsaw.

3 Using a dry erase marker, I created my lettering. The marks remove very easily from acrylic with a dry paper towel in case you make a mistake. With wood, use a light pencil mark.

4 Then I placed an X at each point the wire needed to thread through. Script lettering is ideal because it curves and connects better than print.

5a

5b

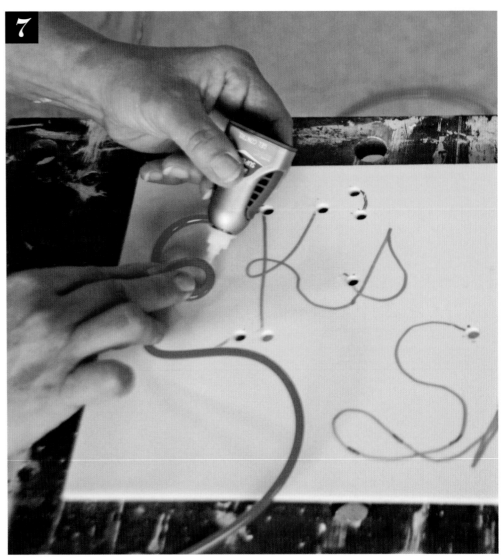

7

5 Using the drill and pilot bit, followed by the ¼″ bit, I drilled through each X to make openings for the wire.

6 Taking the coil of EL wire by the tip, I pushed it up through the first hole and threaded it all the way through until I reached the end that is attached to the battery pack.

7 The wire should follow the curves of each letter. Every few inches, I held the wire in place and dabbed two or three small drops of gel super glue underneath, then pressed carefully for about a minute or two to let it cure. Rub away the marker ink as you go so that it doesn't get trapped under the wire or glue.

8 When finished, I drilled the last hole and pulled the wire to the back of the sign. I wrapped the excess wire in electrical tape and secured it to the acrylic. You can either tape the battery pack to the back of the sign or put it inside the shed for easier access. (You'll need to drill a hole through the wall for this.)

9 To hang the sign, I drilled tiny holes on either end of the sign. I inserted S hooks on both ends of the chain, then put the hooks into the holes and into screw eyes installed underneath the roof.

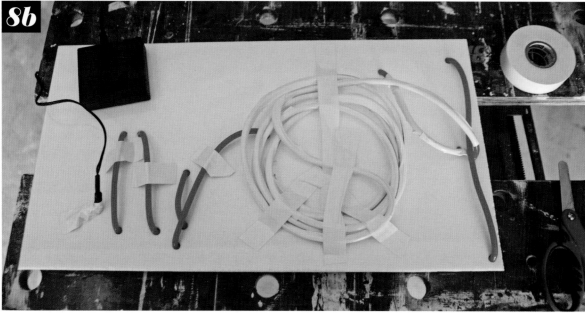

A teal blue canning jar sets off a fun mix of roses and hydrangeas and their country cousins, lavender and thistle.

Floral Arrangements

When it comes to flower arranging in the shed, clusters of small arrangements often work well. They fit on narrow shelves or small tables and can be moved around easily to change up your look. Hillary Black gathered various low-profile containers to create some simple designs. Here are some of her tips and ideas to make your own.

Take clippings from your herb garden or kitchen to add scent and interest. Using a striking combination of pavé roses (clustered closely together at even height) with oregano, variegated sage, and chamomile in the background, Hillary made this unique arrangement that would look terrific anywhere.

A passionate recycler, Hillary found a new use for old water bottles in this whimsical country-meadow bouquet. Repurposing a wood tea box, Hillary placed a cut-off water bottle inside and filled it with some water. Once cut to size, the light plastic is easily manipulated to fit this squared vessel. The cut bottle holds the box top in place, creating a backdrop for the chamomile flowers.

Reminiscent of old photos, tone-on-tone flowers are stunning in their understatement. Hillary combined hydrangeas and Kermit mums in shades of cream and pale green, keeping the vases simple accordingly. Repurpose small vessels such as juice glasses (shown here atop an upside-down votive), small bowls, creamers, and similar items easily found in your cupboard or a thrift shop.

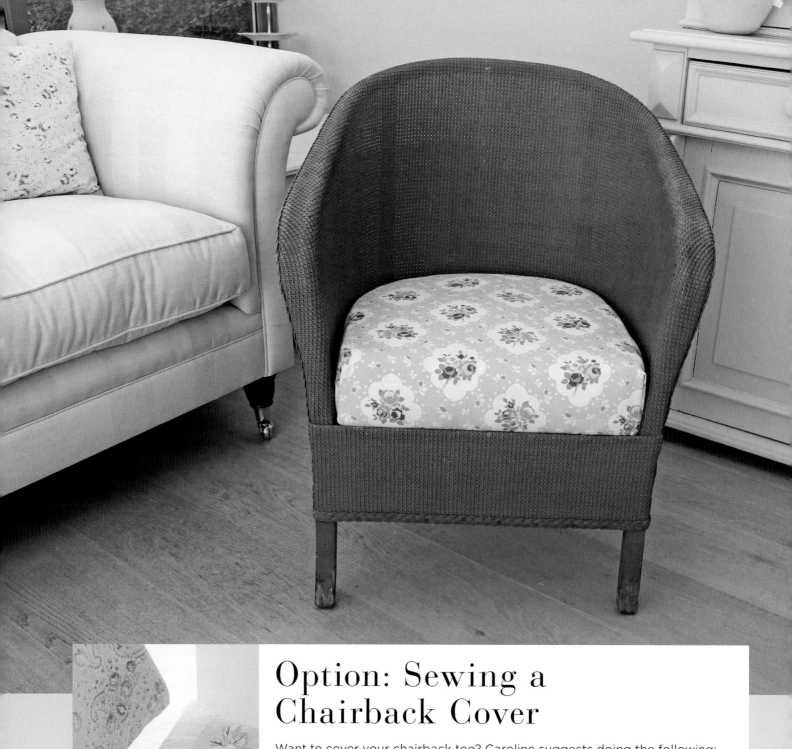

Option: Sewing a Chairback Cover

Want to cover your chairback too? Caroline suggests doing the following: Create a pattern as you did for the seat cushion (see page 169) and cut two fabric pieces, adding a ⅝″ seam allowance. Stitch them right sides together, leaving the bottom side open. Turn right side out and slip over the chairback. Finish the open seam using a slipstitch or fabric glue.

Easy Chair Seat Recover

Make a fresh and pretty office chair or reading chair by recovering the seat and back with new fabric. Whether it's a simple removable seat cushion like the one in Caroline Borgman's demonstration or an office chair as shown here with an additional back support, the process is very straightforward, even for beginners. The magic tool here is a staple gun; find one at fabric, craft, or hardware stores.

Materials

- Fabric chalk
- Scrap fabric
- Seat fabric
- Staples

Tools

- Eye and ear protection
- Work gloves
- Tape measure
- Scissors
- Staple gun

1 Caroline started by measuring the length and width of the seat pad and adding on the height/drop of the sides of the seat pad, plus an additional 1" hem allowance.

2 She then took the dimensions and chalked out a curved-shape template onto some scrap fabric. (The shape doesn't have to be exact, as you can cut away excess fabric.)

3 She drew around the scrap template onto the main fabric and cut it out.

4 Next, she laid out the main fabric, right side down, and placed the seat pad upside down on top of it.

5 Caroline smoothed out the fabric and secured the center back (curved) seat shape with one staple underneath the seat pad.

6 At this point, she pulled the fabric taut and added a staple to the center front underneath the pad. Then, keeping the fabric taut, she stapled underneath the seat pad base, starting with the curves. Caroline worked to get just three folds on each side to create a smooth curve. She turned and folded the front corners and stapled the fabric underneath the seat pad. She continued stapling all the way around, keeping the fabric as smooth as possible and cutting away excess fabric as necessary.

7 Caroline used her scrap fabric to finish off the bottom so that the springs wouldn't show, but this step is optional.

8 Once finished, Caroline turned over the pad and placed it back into the chair.

She Shed Space Plan

You've made it to the final page. I'm thinking you're ready to jump from dream to reality, right? Nothing makes your plans more concrete than a design on paper or onscreen. A space plan (also called a floor plan) moves your pretty-but-vague ideas into the real world of size and configuration. You can draw a plan by hand, using pencil and ruler, or with any number of online space plan apps.

Below is a sample space plan for a 11' x 19.5' she shed. Use this, as well as the short checklist below, to begin building your own space. It will make your planning and building much more efficient—fewer mistakes, better buying decisions.

She Shed Checklist

- Usage: How will I be using my she shed? (lounging, writing, painting, working, entertaining)
- Wall measurements
- Door size, placement, and swing radius
- Windows: Width, height, distance from floor, swing radius (if they open)
- Key furnishings (sofa, desk, worktable, chairs, bookshelves, cabinets)
- Furnishings measurements
- Walking and movement space (ideally 2' between cabinet and sofa back, 3' clearance near main entrance, 1' between chair and coffee table)

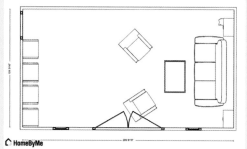

A space plan for your she shed is essential for helping you figure out what you need and whether everything is going to fit into your shed. It will also help you place your windows and door and is a great help when you're sourcing your flooring and furnishings.

Acknowledgments

We talk a lot about community these days; even though we aren't barn raising and hand plowing anymore, we need the strength of teamwork more than ever. This book is bound together with the support, ideas, hard work, and enthusiasm of a she shed community that is growing larger every day.

I was very fortunate in having a team of pros at my side while writing this book. Rebecca Ittner, longtime friend and former *Romantic Homes/Victorian Homes* colleague, lent her keen eye as primary photographer for most of the sheds featured in these pages. No shot was too difficult, even if it meant squeezing herself halfway in and halfway out of a shed window. Hillary Black, gifted stylist and floral advisor, made ordinary objects extraordinary with her theatrical flair. Together the three of us enjoyed the photographic journeys and formed new friendships with the she shed owners.

Undying gratitude goes to my husband and biggest fan, Timothy Hayes. After the first book, he swore he'd never work on another she shed. Yet, there he was last summer, sharing his precious tools with me to build my own shed and helping me design many of the projects seen in this book. Every time I stopped him, midcut, to wait for a photo, I made a mental tally mark on my IOU sheet.

Thank you to Hillary Black, Caroline Borgman, Kim Brandstater, Sabrina Contreras, Carla Fisher, Deborah Hayes, Kathy Hurwitz, Rebecca Ittner, Ellen Marcus, Nina McNamar, Dana and Sean O'Brien, Liz Ridgway, and Jeff and Lynn Robson for contributing your wonderful creative projects to the book.

She shed owners are some of the most giving and community-minded women I've ever met. They've created their sanctuaries and they share them so that others can create theirs too. They are the real deal and I am privileged to belong to this happy group.

Resources

p. 18, 31, 85: Rachel Roe Design; www.rachelroedesign.com

p. 26, 80: Jane Ashmore's beach hut; www.thelittlebeachhutcompany.co.uk

p. 40: A Place to Grow/ Recycled Greenhouses; www.recycledgreenhouses.com

p. 44, 48, 71: Nina McNamar, Creative Farm Girl; www.creativefarmgirl.com

p. 52, 136, 156: Deborah Hayes; www.mileyrosecreations.com

p. 56, 64: She Shades Paints; www.sheshadespaints.com

p. 59, 83: Ali Ferguson, textile artist; www.aliferguson.co.uk

p. 84: Tackable wallcoverings; www.fabricmate.com, www.koroseal.com (to the trade only)

p. 93: Carol Cook, Art and Sand; www.artandsand.blogspot.com

p. 104: IOD Decor Stamps; www.ironorchiddesigns.com

p. 140: Lavender Marketplace & Workshops; www.lavenderworkshops.com

p. 144: Christine Darnell Gardens; www.christinedarnellgardens.com

p. 155: Hanging planters; www.urban-flowers.co.uk

p. 160: Denys & Fielding; www.denysandfielding.co.uk

p. 162: EL wire; www.glowcity.com

p. 168: Caroline Borgman Interior Design; www.carolineborgman.co.uk

p. 171: Space plan; www.2beesinapod.com

Photo Credits

2 Bees in a Pod: 171

Caroline Hayes: 24, 25 (top)

Christine Darnell: 144

Deborah Hayes: 52, 54-55 (all), 138-139 (all), 156-157 (all)

Elizabeth Hayes: 16 (bottom), 65 (both), 126 (right), 155 (top right), 168 (top), 169 (all),

Erika Kotite: 25 (bottom), 39 (middle), 107, 108 (top three), 109 (both), 134-135 (all), 163, 164-165 (all)

Everton Shed/Costco: 17 (bottom)

GAP Interiors: 6 (Colin Poole), 26 (Richard Gadsby), 59 (Douglas Gibb), 80 (Richard Gadsby), 83 (Douglas Gibb), 115 (Colin Poole), 168 inset (Colin Poole)

Hillary Black: 3, 87, 166

Jirapa Cocking: 127

John Sutton Photography: 32 (top), 118 (landscape architect: Scott Lewis Landscape Architecture)

Kloter Farms: 19 (top), 39 (bottom)

Lynn Robson: 128-129 (all), 130-131 (all),

Natalie Ramsay/Liz Ridgway: 160-161

Nina McNamar: 44-45 (all), 46-47 (all), 48, 50-51 (all), 72-73 (all),

Rachel Roe: 10 (top), 18 (both), 20, 31 (right), 85, 153 (right), 155 (bottom right)

Rebecca Ittner: front cover, back cover, 4, 9, 10 (bottom), 11 (both), 12, 13, 14, 16 (top), 17 (top), 19 (bottom), 22, 28, 29, 30 (both), 31 (left), 32, 33 (all), 34, 35, 36, 38 (both), 39 (top), 40, 42-43 (all), 56, 62, 64, 66, 67, 68, 70 (all), 74-75 (all), 76-77 (both), 78-79 (all), 84 (both), 86, 88, 89, 90, 91, 92, 93, 94 (both), 95 (all), 96-97 (all), 98, 100-101 (all), 102-103 (all), 104-105 (all), 106, 110, 112-113 (all), 114 (both), 116, 119, 120, 121, 122, 123, 124, 125, 132, 134-135 (all), 136, 140-141 (both), 142-143 (all), 146, 148, 149 (both), 150, 151, 152, 153 (left), 154, 155 (left), 158-159 (all), 162, 167 (all), 170 (both), 176

Rebecca Lynne Spencer: 60 (both), 126 (left)

Richard Wells: 37

Sandy Foster: 23

Shutterstock: 108 (bottom right)

Index

About the Author

Erika Kotite is a home and lifestyle expert, and the author of *She Sheds: A Room of Your Own*. She is the co-founder of She Shed Living, a gathering space for women who enjoy life in their backyards, and She Shades, a line of chalk-based exterior paints. The former editor of *Romantic Homes* and *Victorian Homes*, Erika worked for years as a partner in a book-packaging company, editing and developing books within the arts, textile, and crafting sectors. Some of her other book projects include *Blogging for Bliss*, *Natural Soapmaking*, *Natural Candlemaking*, *Photo Album Quilts*, *Felt Fashion*, and *The Daily Book of Photography*. Erika has been interviewed by and featured in *Architectural Digest*, Buzzfeed, Oprah.com, *Parents*, *Toronto Sun*, *Orange County Register*, NBC's *Today Show*, PBS' *Central Texas Gardener*, and Toronto City TV's *Breakfast TV* show. Erika lives in Huntington Beach, California, with her husband and three children.